Collectible Paint Advertising and Memorabilia

Irene Davis

Schiffer Publishing Ltd
4880 Lower Valley Road, Atglen, PA 19310 USA

Dedication

I would like to dedicate this to my husband, who has continually encouraged me to look for paint cans and advertising. His help with this book, getting the items cleaned and ready for photos has been endless. I would not have attempted this project without him. However, the one who has really made this book possible, is the "Keeper of the Stars". This book on paint collectibles has been in the planning stages for many years...in God's book. It was no accident that Carter and I met; God had a hand in it long before we even knew.

Disclaimer

This book has not been authorized by any paint companies or manufacturers. The author claims no ownership of any of the copyrights, trademarks or names of any companies used in this book. The book has been compiled as a way to preserve the history of paint advertising for paint companies across the country.

The prices in this book are guides only and author makes no guarantee of their accuracy. They are average and they may vary widely by area, condition, supply, and demand.

Library of Congress Catalog Card Number: 99-67493

Book Design by Anne Davidsen
Type set in Copperplate Gothic / Souvenir Light

ISBN: 0-7643-1047-X

Printed in China
1 2 3 4

Published by Schiffer Publishing Ltd.
4880 Lower Valley Road
Atglen, PA 19310
Phone: (610) 593-1777
Fax: (610) 593-2002
Please visit out web site catalog at
www.schifferbooks.com
or write for a free catalog.
This book may be purchased from the publisher.
Please include $3.95 for shipping.

In Europe, Schiffer books are distributed by
Bushwood Books
6 Marksbury Ave.
Kew Gardens
Surrey TW9 4JF England
Phone: 44 (0)208 392-8585
Fax: 44 (0)208 392-9876
E-mail: Bushwd@aol.com

Please try your bookstore first.

We are interested in hearing from authors
with book ideas on related subjects.

Table of Contents

Introduction

History

Is it older than dirt? Almost. In fact, paint is about 30,000 years old. Graphics done with crude paint were left behind by cavemen. However, it was not until the 1700s that the first paint mill was built in America by Thomas Child in Boston, Massachusetts.

The next big step was taken in the mid 1800s when the first paint factories started arriving on the scene. D. R. Averill of Ohio was given the first patent on "Ready Mixed" paints, however, this new type of paint was not well received.

Henry Alden Sherwin, one of the partners of Sherwin, Dunham, and Griswold wanted to let homeowners choose their own premixed colors.

He also believed that factory paint should be of higher quality and better consistency. Unfortunately, his ideas were not well received by his partners and the partnership dissolved. Mr. Sherwin's ideas must have sounded interesting to Edward Williams, and they formed a new company by the name of Sherwin-Williams.

Sherwin-Williams spent ten years working on this new formula. Finally in 1880 they succeeded by coming up with a quality paint that surpassed everything on the market. People no longer needed to mix lead base, linseed oil, turpentine and paint pigments to get paint...it was now all premixed in a can. Up to that time, a "professional" painter had to be hired to mix this secret formula; now painting was a do-it-yourself procedure.

The Industrial Revolution was creating a new market for their paint. Products from the Model T Ford to televisions needed paints and coatings. A painting frenzy had been created. Everything needed paint, from mouldings to furniture, from homes to wagons. The demand grew for this premixed paint, and many small to medium manufacturers sprang up to serve their local buying area.

In the 1950s the use of lead pigments started to be limited because of potential risk. In 1978 the Consumer Products Safety Commission banned the use of any lead in household paint.

As with other industries, small and medium sized companies either were purchased by larger companies or just went out of business. At the present, there are more than 1000 manufacturers, most of who are primarily concerned with architectural coatings (i.e., house paint). The idea of ready-mixed paint was definitely a successful one.

Collecting Paint Cans & Advertising

Paint signs, thermometers, and giveaways have been collected for many years. They have been included in many books and price guides. I love these items and have included many examples in this book. However, paint cans, for whatever reason, have been overlooked. Like any collectible, they are part of our history and reflect our changing times.

Automobiles, furniture, interior design and style can be seen on labels of early paint cans. In addition to the larger name brand companies, there were many smaller local companies throughout the country, so the search for different brand paints and labels can be endless. These advertised to the consumer an image of what their freshly painted items would look like, and the logos—which were works of art—showed lavish colors and detailed designs.

Full, mint gallon cans are much harder to find than smaller cans. Gallon cans were opened, and paint spilled over the edges. They were stored in damp outbuildings, and eventually thrown away. Gallon cans take a lot of space to display and may prohibit you from collecting a lot of these, however, include one or two of these in your collection. Look for a colorful labels with detailed graphics.

Small cans are still plentiful. They were purchased for touch-ups or small jobs, then stored under the counter for future use. Because of the smaller size, the graphics may not be as detailed; however, their size is appealing.

Paint can collecting is fresh and affordable. They can be found at yard sales, flea markets or antique shops; it is rare that I go out and don't come back with an old paint can. Look for unusual shapes, sizes, and graphics. Mint, unused cans with colorful, complex graphics are the most desirable but will cost you more. They display well along side any collectible advertising...from coffee tins to duck decoys. After all, paint is found on almost everything. Happy Hunting!

Price and Condition

Paint can collecting is a new field and there is no "history" to pricing. Determining the fair price for a paint can is not easy. You are dealing with a new collectible area, and there is a wide range of graphics, colors, and sizes. The prices shown in this book reflect the condition of the can in the photo. If you have an item you do not see in this book, it does not mean it's rare or common, it just means you have a different paint can. Paint cans and advertising are over 100 years old and since each company had a different label for each product, the variety of cans and advertising is endless.

Dating paint cans can be hard. The style of furniture or the year of automobile on the label may give you some indication of the approximate era. Sometimes, dates can be found by researching literature given to the retailers. However, for the most part, it is extemely hard to date paint memorabilia. Small companies did a minimal amount of advertising and had no literature. Also, they either went out of business or were bought by larger companies, so their records have vanished.

Cans that have labels with many colors, detailed graphics and odd shapes, will command the highest prices. The lowest-priced cans will be the ones with only one or two colors on their labels, no graphics, and regular shapes.

Unlike the cans, paint advertising—such as signs, thermometers and giveaways—has been collected for many years. The marketplace has established prices on much of it. Once again, the price shown reflects the items in the photo. Be prepared to pay more or less depending on condition and your wants.

Many people take prices shown in a price guide too seriously. Paint cans and advertising still show up everywhere, so make it fit into your pocketbook and your lifestyle. Display it, enjoy it and if you buy a full can of paint, you may even use it someday!

Standard Condition Terms

Mint in box (MIB): Item is in mint condition with original wrapper or box.

Mint: New condition, perhaps old store stock, no marks or scratches visible.

Near Mint (NM): Might appear mint, however, it may show some minor marks or a tiny tear.

Excellent (exc.): Only minor problems, such as some tiny flaking and slight fading; could have a small dent or tear but not in the main advertising itself.

Good: It has small dents, scratches, pitting, fading, and rust. Still displayable and enjoyable.

Poor: Many faults, and unless it is given to you, perhaps should be passed.

Correspondence

Irene Davis, P.O. Box 63, New Church, Virginia 23415; or contact her at her web site:
www.creekhouseantiques.com.

Chapter One

Paint Cans & Containers

General Paints & Varnishes

Everwhite Enamel. Ohio Varnish Co., printed litho label, quart $250; gallon size, late 1930s, $400.

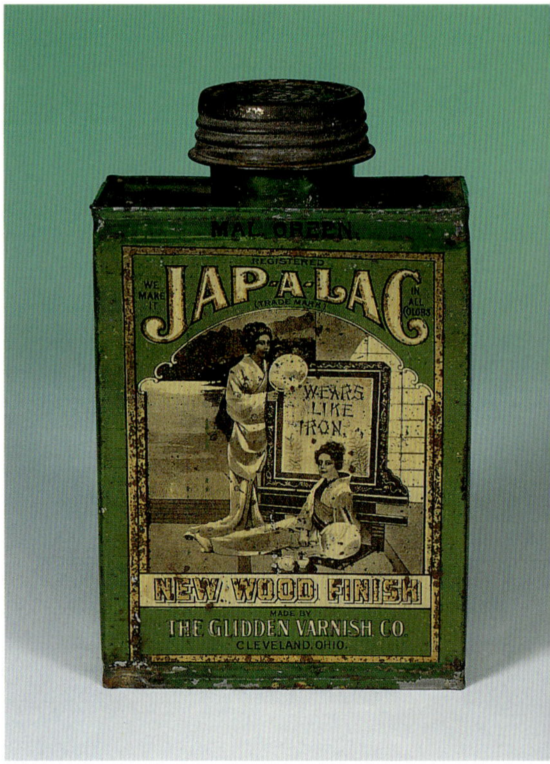

Jap-A-Lac. The Glidden Varnish Co., printed litho label, 3.25" x 6", 1920s, $175.

Jap-A-Lac. The Glidden Varnish Co., opener attached to top, mixing powder container on the bottom, paper label, 3" x 2.5", $65.

Bruin Paint. Baer Brothers, paper label, gallon size $125.

Floorene. The American Varnish Company, printed litho label, 1/4-gallon size, $95.

Stag Semi-Paste Paint. Hirshberg Paint Co., applied paper label, 5-gallon size, $175.

Thomas Paint. A. H. Thomas Paint Co., applied paper label, gallon size, $75.

Tiger White Lead. The Steel Company of Canada Limited, bucket style 7" x 7", printed litho label, $150.

Left to right: Baer's Klondike Size 25; Baer Brothers, paper label, screw-off top, $35. Baer's Klondike Size 70; Baer Brothers, paper label, screw-off top, $35. Baer's Spar Aluminum Liquid; applied paper label, 1-pint size, $35. Baer's Klondike Gold Paint; Baer Brothers, paper label, 1-pint size, $25. Baer's Klondike Size 40; Baer Brothers, paper label, screw-off top, $35.

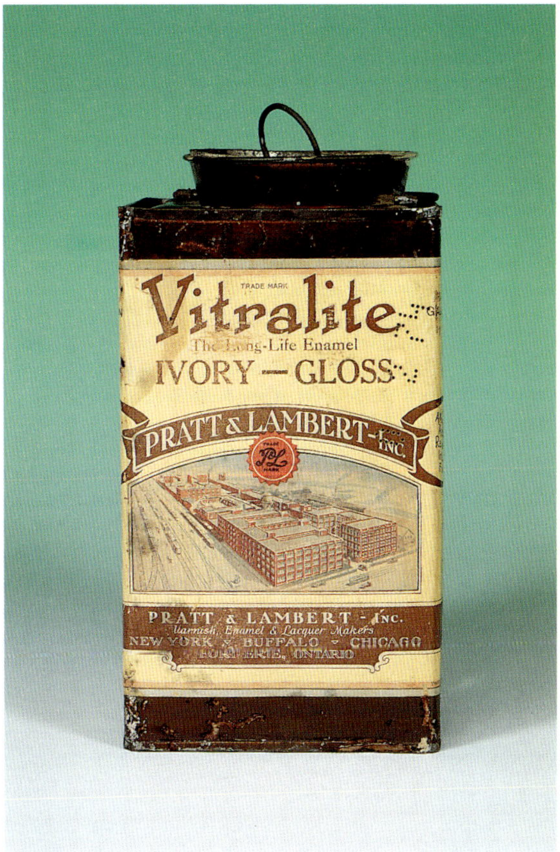

Vitralite. Pratt & Lambert, painted square can, applied paper label, 1/2-gallon size, $125.

McDougall-Butler Varnish. McDougall-Butler Co. Inc., painted with applied paper label, quart size, $50.

Above: Masury 4-hour Enamel. John W. Masury & Son, paper label, 1/2-pint size, $15.

Left: Gilt Edge. Farwell, Ozmun, Kirk & Co., paper with applied paper label, pint size, $50.

Left to right: O'Brien's Enamel; O'Brien Varnish Company, printed label, 1/2-pint size, $15. Pyramid Brand; O'Brien Varnish Company, with applied paper label, screw-off top, pint size, $65. O'Brien's Floor Enamel; O'Brien Varnish Company, paper label, pint size, $30.

Left: Bay State Varnishes; Wadsworth, Howland & Co., square can, printed litho label, gallon size, $25. Right: Bay State Liquid Paint; Wadsworth, Howland & Co., round can, printed litho label, 1/2-gallon size, $60.

Left: Gibbsboro Prussian Blue; John Lucas & Co., paper label, 1/4-pint size, $15. Right: John Lucas & Co., applied paper label, 1/2-gallon size, $65.

Lucas. John Lucas & Co., paper label. 1/4-pint size, $10; 1/2-pint size, $10; 1/4-pint size, $10.

Left to right: Cook's Rapidry Enamel; Cook Paint & Varnish Co., paper label, pint size, $20; paper label, 4-ounce size, $15. Cook's Pure Orange Shellac; Cook Paint & Varnish Co., paper label, pint size, $15.

Left to right: Enamel-Kote; Acme Quality Paints, Inc., paper label, 1/4-pint size, $15. Penetrating Oil Stain; Acme Quality Paints, Inc., paper label, 1/4-pint size, $15. Enamel-Kote; Acme Quality Paints, Inc., paper label, 1/2-pint size, $15; 1/2-pint size, $15.

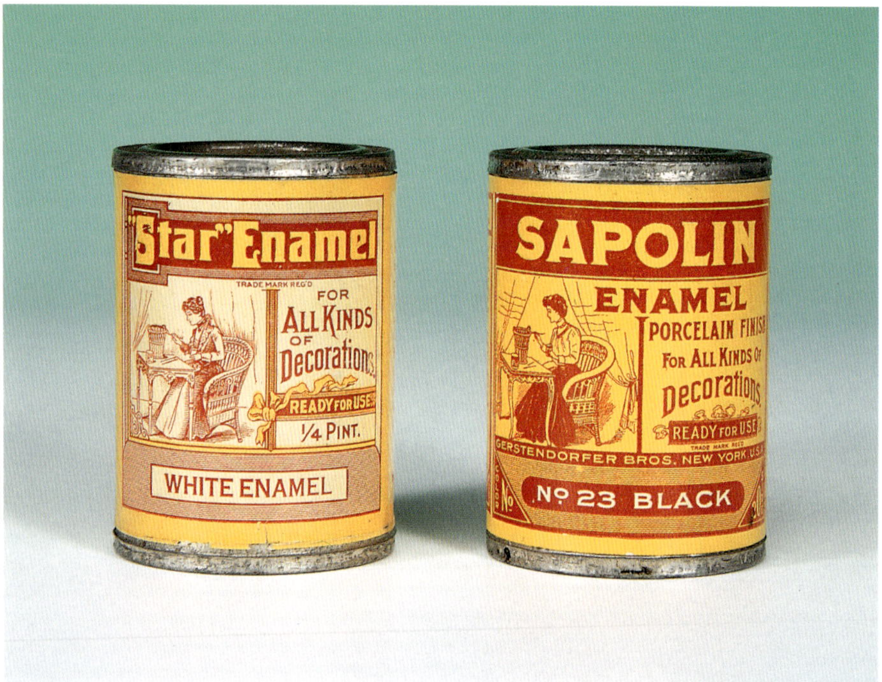

Left: Star Enamel; Gerstendorfer Bros., paper label, 1/4-pint size, $25. Right: Sapolin Enamel; Gerstendorfer Bros., paper label, 1/4-pint size, $25.

Left to right: BPS Blackboard Slating; The Patterson-Sargent Co., paper label, 1/2-pint, $10. Flatlux; The Patterson-Sargent Co., printed litho label, quart size, $15. BPS Interior Bronzing Liquid; The Patterson-Sargent Co., applied paper label, pint size, $35. BPS Aluminum Enamel; The Patterson-Sargent Co., paper label 1/8-pint size, $10.

Left: LiqUidEne Decorative Enamel; Yarnall Paint Co., paper label, 1/16-gallon size, $25. Right: LiqUidEne Varnish Stain; Yarnall Paint Co., paper label, 1/16-gallon size, $25.

McCloskey. McCloskey Varnish Co., paper label, pint size, $25; quart size, $40.

Han:Bro:Lyte. Hanline Bros., paper label, pint size, $15.

Glidden Paint. The Glidden Co., paper labels, quart size, $5; gallon size, $10.

Parisian Scarlet. Thomas W. Cook & Co., oval shape, applied paper label, 6" x 3.5", $35.

Breinig's Allentown Paint. Allentown Paint Mfg. Co., applied paper label, gallon size, $45.

Jiffy-Namel. Felton Sibley & Co. Inc., paper label, 1/4-pint size, $15; 1/2-pint size, $15.

Left: Baronial Rapid Dry Enamel; Republic Paint & Varnish Co., paper label, pint size, $15. Right: Republic Paints; Republic Paint & Varnish Co., paper label, quart size, $5.

Pitkin's Barn Paint. Geo. W. Pitkin Co., applied paper label, gallon size, $25.

Left: Red Devil Quick Drying Enamel; Technical Color & Chemical Works, Inc., paper label, quart size, $15. Right: Red Devil Enamel; Red Devil Paints & Chemicals, Division of Insilco, printed litho label, quart size, $10.

Vita-Lux Enamel. Vita-Var Corporation, paper label, 1/32-gallon size, $15; pint size, $15.

Sapolin Paints, Inc. Top Row: Porcelain Gloss Finish, paper label, 1/4-pint size, $20. Mel-Lux, Satin Alkyd Enamel, paper label, quart size, $15. Master Painter's Fluid Oil, paper label, 1/8-pint size, $20. Mel-Lux, Satin Alkyd Enamel, paper label, quart size, $15. Radiator & Range Enamel, paper label, 1/2-pint, $20. Bottom Row: Custom Mix, paper label, 3 5/8-quart size, $15. Professional Finish, Alkyd Flat, paper label, gallon size, $15. Rubber Base Coating, paper label, gallon size, $15.

Socony Paints. Socony Paint Products Company (A Socony Mobil Company), paper label, gallon size, $45.

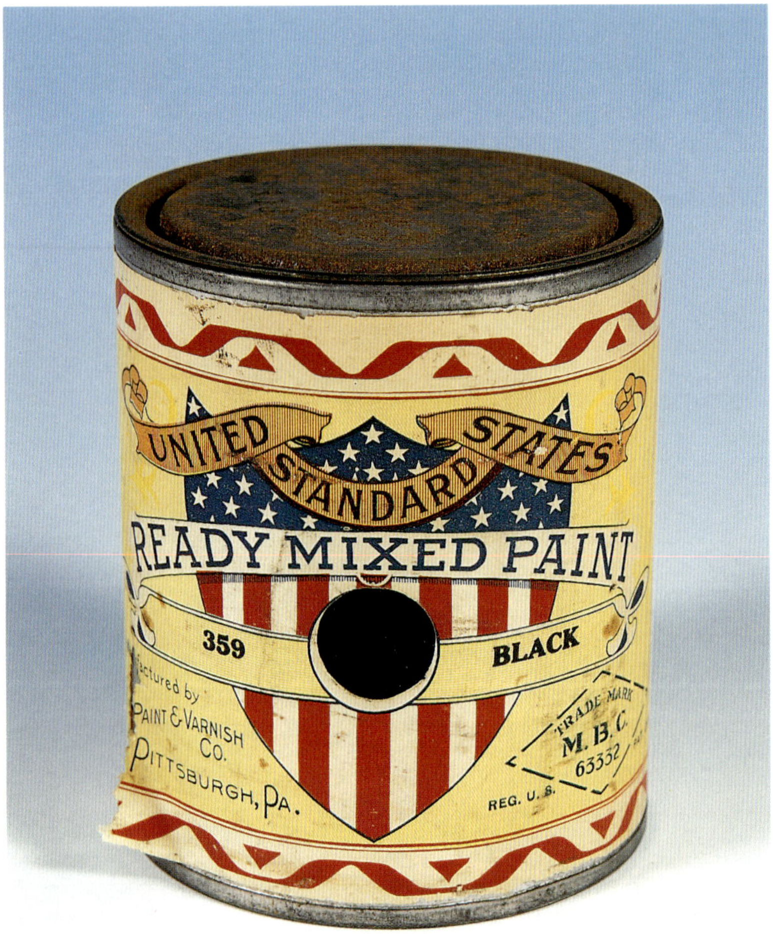

United States Standard Ready Mixed Paints, paper label, quart size, $45.

Colors in Oil. Benjamin Moore & Co., paper label, 1/2-pint size, $10.

Ornaline Household Paint. Banner Paint & Varnish Co., paper label, 1/2-pint size, $15.

Pittsburgh Plate Glass Company, clockwise from top: Waterspar Enamel, paper label, 1/16-gallon size, $25. Waterspar Enamel, paper label, $10. Wallhide Semi-Gloss Enamel, paper label, quart size, $10. Wallhide Flat Wall Paint, paper label, gallon size, $35. Satinhide Enamel, paper label, quart size, $10.

Left: The Sherwin-Williams Co. Chrome Finish, paper label, 1/2-pint size, $10. Right: A-100 Latex House Paint Repaint Additive, paper label, pint size, $10.

Oriole Lead and Zinc. August Miller & Son, applied paper label, gallon size, $45.

Kalamazoo Mastic Mixed Paints. Kalamazoo Mastic Paint Works, applied paper label, 1/2-gallon size, $25.

Lus-Tro-Lac. Colonial Works, paper label, quart size, $50.

Atlaslac. Geo. D. Wetherill & Co., paper label, quart size, $95.

Devoe Zinc Dust Primer and Finish. Devoe & Raynolds Company, Inc., paper label, quart size, $35.

Peerless Prepared Paint. The A. Wilhelm Co., paper label, 1/24-gallon size, $5; 1/8-gallon size, $15.

Tom Thumb 4 Hour Enamel. Chicago Paints, Inc., paper label, 3.65 ounce size, $5.

Ripolin. The Ripolin Company, paper label, 1/8-gallon size, $25.

Little Trojan Four Hour Enamel. The Tredennick Paint Mfg. Co., paper label, 1/36-gallon size, $20.

Ak-Sar-Ben Varnish. Reifschneider Paint & Glass Co., paper label, quart size, $30.

Left: McQuade Trim Colors; John McQuade & Co., paper label, quart size, $15.
Right: McQuade Interior Gloss; John McQuade & Co., paper label, gallon size, $25.

Left to right: Cook's Paint and Varnish, 1 1/2-pint size, screw-off top, $25 each. Midland Prepared Paint, quart size, $12.

Best Colors In Oil. Heath & Milligan Mfg. Co., paper label, $15.

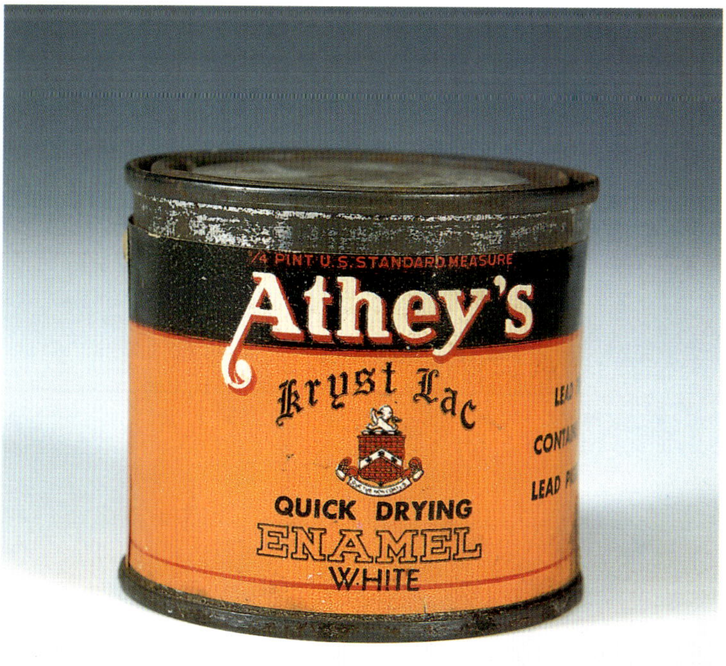

Athey's Krust Lac Quick Drying Enamel. The C. M. Athey Paint Co., paper label, 1/4-pint size, $5.

Par-O-Keet Lacquer. The Lowe Brothers Company, paper label, 1/2-pint size, $35.

Kresge Varnish Stain. S.S. Kresge Co., paper label, 1/10-gallon size, $10.

Above: Per-Ma-Lite Four Hour Enamel. George M. Budeke Co., paper label, 1/2-pint size, $15.

Left: Penco 4 Hour Enamel. J.C. Penney Co., paper label, 1/4-pint size, $25.

Nu-Enamel. Nu-Enamel Corporation, paper label, 1/8-pint size, $15.

Kolorful Quick Dry Enamel. City Paint Co., paper label, 1/36-gallon size, $10.

Crow Black Enamel. Frank Bownes Company, Inc., 1/4-pint size, $35.

Eagle Pure White Lead.
The Eagle-Picher Lead Company,
printed litho label, 60 lbs. $125.

Dutch Boy Heavy Paste White Lead. National Lead Company, 25 lbs., $35.

Stag Semi-Paste Paint. Hirshberg Paint Co., applied paper label, gallon size, $75.

Dutch Boy All-Purpose White Lead. National Lead Company, printed litho label, 50 lbs. $35.

Dutch Boy Red Lead. National Lead Company, printed litho label, $25.

Left to right: Dutch Boy Lead Mixing Oil; National Lead Company, applied paper label, 1/4-gallon, $15. Dutch Boy White Lead, litho printed label, 1 lb., $15. Sash & Trim Colors; paper label, quart size, $10. Dutch Boy Soft Paste White Lead; litho printed label, 25 lbs., price includes lid shown in photo, $75.

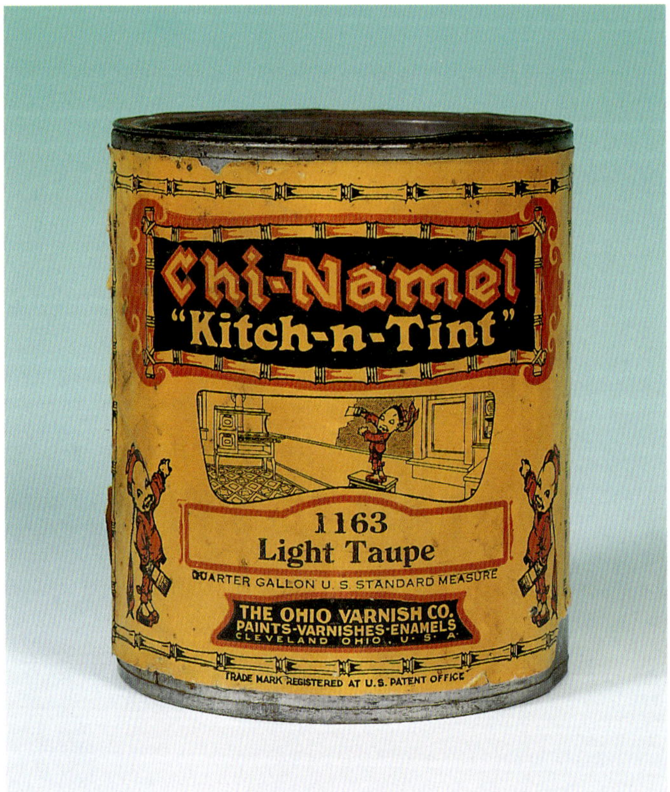

Chi-Namel Kitch-n-Tint, The Ohio Varnish Co., paper label, quart size, $45.

Carter White Lead Company, decal label, 25 lbs., $40.

Floorene. The American Varnish Co., gallon size, $175.

Blue Ridge High Gloss Enamel. Blue Ridge Talc Co., Inc., Paint Division, paper label, quart size, $10.

Super Valspar. Valentine & Co., paper label, 1/4-pint size, $10.

Tungee Enamel. Tungee Enamel & Varnish Corp., paper label, 1/4-pint size, $25.

Luxalak 4-Hour Enamel. Baker's, paper label, $10.

Glos-Tone. The Martin-Senour Co., paper label, 1/16-gallon size, $25.

Dinah Black Enamel, Boston Varnish Company, Left to right: Paper label, 1/4-pint size, $85. Glass jar with paper label, 1/4-pint size, $60; quart size, $225; 1/2-pint size, $125.

Satin-Glo Enamel, British America Paint Co. Ltd. Left to Right: Paper label, 3-ounce size, $50; 1/14 gallon size, $45; 1/4-gallon size, $75 each.

Left: Kyanize White Enamel; Boston Varnish Company, applied paper label, 1/2-pint size, $90. Right: Kyanize Celoid Finish; Boston Varnish Company, applied paper label, 1/2-pint size, $125.

Kyanize White Enamel. Boston Varnish Company, applied paper label, gallon size, $125.

Specialty Paints & Varnishes

McDougall-Butler Varnish. McDougall-Butler Co. Inc., applied paper label, gallon size, $35.

Regatta Vinyltex 59. Jotum-Baltimore Copper Paint Co., paper label, quart size, $30.

Racing Compound. Tarr & Wonson, Ltd., paper label, gallon size, $50.

Z-Spar Monopoxy. Andrew Brown Co., paper label, quart size, $30.

Man O'War Ultra Spar Marine Varnish. McCloskey Varnish Co., printed litho label, 1/2-pint size, $25.

Top: Homer Brand Sign Painters Supplies; Riker's Sales Service, applied paper label, $15. Bottom Row: Fibroseal Bulletin Colors; Hooker Glass & Paint Mfg. Co., paper label, 1/2-pint size, $15. Kem Bulletin Colors, The Sherwin-Williams Co., paper label, quart size, $15. Graphic Arts, The Sherwin-Williams Co., paper label, pint size, $15.

Left: Black Asphalt Paint; The Philip-Carey Co., printed litho label, sample, $10. Right: Varnishes Black Arphaltum; The A. Burdsal Co., paper label, quart size, $15.

Left: Burdsal's Cement Primer; The A. Burdsal Company, paper label, quart size, $10. Right: Medusa Portland Cement Paint, Medusa Portland Cement Co., printed litho label, gallon size, $50.

Left: Marietta Finishes; The Marietta Paint & Color Company, paper label, quart size, $10. Right: Rutland Roof Coating. Rutland Fire Clay Co., printed litho label, gallon size, $75.

Left: Bikenamel; Western Auto Supply Co., paper label, 1/4-pint size, $10. Right: Schwinn Cycle Enamel; Edward E. Allen Mfg. Co., paper label, 1/4-pint size, $15.

Burdsal's Old Mission Wood Stain; The A. Burdsal Company, paper label, pint size, $10. Stag Wood Stain, The Hirsherg Paint Co., paper label, pint size, $25.

Steelcote Rubber Enamel; Steelcote Manufacturing Company, printed litho label, 1/4-pint size, $20; pint size, $35; 1/2-pint size, $35.

Left to right: Superior Quality Bronze Powder; Till Paint Co., paper label, 1/2-lb. can, $10. Pittsburgh Bronze Powders; Pittsburgh Plate Glass Company, paper label, 1 lb. can, $10. Fixall Gold Bronze; Louisville Varnish Co., paper label (2-part can), 1/4-pint size, $25.

Left: Marsching's French Gold Paint; two bottles in cardboard box, $75. Right: American Gold Leaf Paint; two bottles in cardboard box, $50.

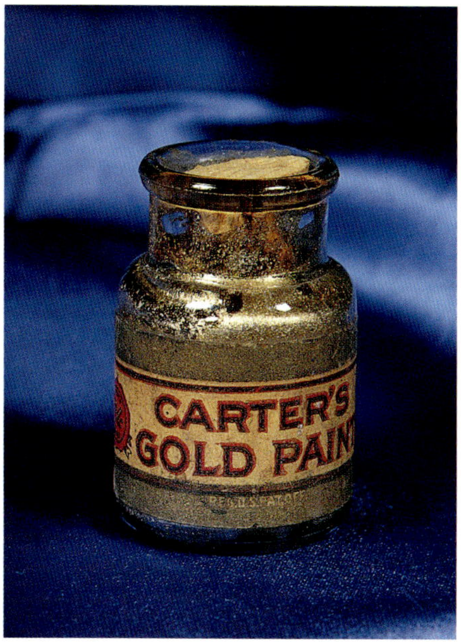

Carter's Gold Paint. Glass bottle with stopper, applied paper label, 2" tall, $15.

Left: Stove Pipe and Iron Enamel; The Sherwin-Williams Co., paper label, 1/2-pint can, $10.
Right: Stove Pipe Enamel; The Tredennick Paint Mfg. Co., paper label, 7/64-gallon can, $15.

Left to right: Bright Wagon Paint; John Lucas & Co., Inc., paper label, quart size, $65. Wagon and Implement Paint; Colonial Works, applied paper label, 1/8-gallon can, $65. Tractor Paint; Geo. D. Wetherill & Co., Inc., paper label, quart size, $65.

Left to right: Air Dry Acrylic; Harley-Davidson Motor Co. Inc., paper label, quart size, $45. Spray Paint; AMF Harley Davidson Motor Co. Inc., paper label, 5.75-ounce can, $15. Quick Drying Enamel; Harley-Davidson Motor Co. Inc., paper label, quart size, $25.

Left to right: Peerless Iron Enamel; Nickel Plate Polish Co., paper label, 1/2-pint can, $15. Hot Pipe Aluminum; Sapolin Co. Inc., paper label, 1/4-pint can, $10. Peerless Iron Enamel; Nickel Plate Polish Co., printed litho label, 1/2-pint can, $15.

Front: Colors in Oil; The Lowe Brothers Company, tube container, printed label, $5. Back, left to right: Yellow Multiple Marking Paint; The Glidden Co., paper label, 4-ounce can, $5. A.C.M.; Arthur C. Mangel Industries, paper label, 1/4-pint can, $5. Carter's Gold Paint; The Carter's Ink Co., wood container, applied paper label, $25. Mobil; Valdura Coatings Division, Socony Paint Products Company, paper label, quart size, $15.

Devoe Wagon and Implement Paint. Devoe & Raynolds & Co., paper label, pint size, $25.

Left to right: Pratt's Roost Paint; Pratt Food Company, printed litho label, 2-ounce size, $25. Carbola, The Modern Disinfecting Whitewash; Carbola Chemical Co., 5-pound cardboard container, $25. Catlett's Kilstain; metal container, $25.

Left: Utility Enamel; Pittsburgh Plate Glass Company, paper label, 1/16-gallon can, $10. Right: Bruin Wire Screen Enamel; Baer Bros., paper label, pint size, $20.

Canvak Canvas Paint. The Buckeye Fabric Finishing Co., printed litho label, gallon size, $65.

Unico Products Super Barn Paint. United Cooperative Inc., printed litho label, 5-gallon can, $125.

Nite-Brite Luminous Paint. United Gilsonite Laboratories, 1 1/2-ounce milk glass bottle, paper label, $5.

Left to right: The Langry Gold Paint Co.; glass bottle with cork stopper, embossed, 2.5", $20. Hat Brite; The Sherwin-Williams Co., glass bottle with pull-off top, applied paper label, 4.5", $35. Paint and Varnish Markers; The Sherwin-Williams Co., glass bottle, embossed, 2.75", $35.

Hat Brite. The Sherwin-Williams Co., glass bottle with box, applied paper label, 4.5", $65.

Prang Tempera, The Better Showcard Color. The American Crayon Company, paper labels, 16 bottles and wooden case (not shown), $175.

Left: Pactra 'namel, for all plastic models; 12 bottles with box, $75. Right: Pactra Raceway Colors, for racing shells; 6 bottles with box, $35.

Hopalong Cassidy Poster Paint. Glass bottle, metal litho screw top, $35.

Century 3 Way Auto Enamel. American Paint Works, paper label, quart size, $65.

Effecto Auto Enamel. Pratt & Lambert, Inc., paper label, 1/2-pint can, $95; pint can, $95.

Fixall Automobile Finish. Louisville Varnish Co., paper label, pint size, $145.

Wizard Automobile Enamel. Western Auto Supply Co., paper label, 1/2 pint can, $50; pint can, $50.

3 Way Auto Enamel. The Glidden Co., paper label, quart size, $45.

Larkin Superfine Automobile Finishes. Larkin Co. Inc., paper label, quart size, $125.

OK Automotive Finishes. The Sherwin-Williams Co., paper label, pint cans, $25 each.

Left to right: Dulux; E. I. Du Pont De Nemours & Co., Inc. paper label, 1/2-pint can, $15. Dulux; 1/4-pint can, $15; quart size, $15.

Nu-Enamel Automobile Finishes. Nu-Enamel Paint Company, Inc., printed litho label, 12-ounce can, $85.

Waterspar Auto Enamel. Pittsburg Plate Glass Co., paper label, 1/32-gallon can, $25; 1/8-gallon can, $35.

Du Pont 7 Touch-Up Enamel. E. I. Du Pont De Nemours & Co. Inc., printed litho label, screw-off lid, 5-ounce can, $20; paper label, pint size, $25.

Left to right: Good Year Touch Up Enamel; Good Year, printed litho label, 5-ounce can, $10. Cross Country Touch-Up Enamel; Sears Roebuck and Co., printed litho label, brush inside attached to lid, 6-ounce can, $25. All-Weather Touch-Up Enamel; Good Year, printed litho label, 6-ounce can, $15.

Varsity Touch-Up Enamel. Varsity Products Co., printed litho label, brush inside attached to lid, 8 fl. oz., $35.

Left to right: Hudson Touch-Up Lacquer; Hudson Motor Car Company, paper label, 3-ounce size, $25. DL 60 Color Patch Enamel; Ford Motor Co., paper label, 3-ounce size, $15. Color Patch; Ford Motor Co., paper label, 3-ounce size, $10.

Left: Touch-Up Black; Steelcoate Manufacturing Co., printed litho label, 5-ounce can, $25. Right: Touch-Up Enamel; Atlas Supply Company, paper label, 5-ounce can, $15.

Left: Mobo Touch Enamel; John T. Stanley Co., paper label, brush inside attached to lid, 1/2-pint can, $25. Right: Permatex Touch-Up Black; Permatex Company, paper label, brush inside attached to lid, 1/2-pint can, $15.

Left: DeSoto X-Act Match Touch-Up Color; Briggs Manufacturing Co., paper label dated 1949, 1-ounce jar, $15. Right: Plymouth X-Act Match Touch-Up Color; Briggs Manufacturing Co., paper label dated 1949, 1-ounce jar, $15.

Dupli-Color Touch-Up. Dupli-Color Products Co. Inc., paper labels. There were two 1.25-ounce bottles in box. Complete set, $125.

Americolor Touch-Up Paint. American Motors Corporation, paper label, 6-ounce can, $15.

Tire Black. E. I. Du Pont De Nemours & Co., printed litho label, pint cans, $35 each.

Left: Parko Colored Tire Paint; Park Chemical Company, paper label, pint size, $15. Right: Whiz Tyre-Wyte; R. M. Hollingshead Corp., printed litho label, 16-ounce size, $25.

Kar-Nu Auto Re-Finisher. The Kar-Nu Company, paper label, $45.

Left: Masury's Superfine Coach Colors; John W. Masury & Son, paper label, $45. Right: Burdsal's Truck and Tractor Enamel; The A. Burdsal Company, paper label, 1/4-gallon can, $15.

Left to right: Seminole Super Chief Enamel; Chicago Paints, Inc., paper label, 1/2-pint can, $25. Seminole Truck and Tractor Enamel; Chicago Paints, Inc., paper label, gallon can, $50; pint size, $35.

Rubrlustre Auto Finishes. The Glidden Company, paper label, pint can, $25.

Auto Enamel Paint Kit, Sears, Roebuck & Co. Kit includes a quart of enamel, a pint of thinner, a 1/4-pound can of body solder, a tack rag, and an instruction sheet. Complete, $55.

Left: Whiz Rapid Repair Enamel; The R. M. Hollingshead Co., screw-off top, $125. Right: Hudson Approved Lacquer; Hudson Motor Car Company, quart can, $60.

Left: Effecto Auto Black Enamel; Pratt & Lambert Inc., paper label, pint size, $50. Right: Cook & Dunn Aluminum Paint; C & D, paper label, pint size, $15.

Left to right: Reflexalite Zinc Enamel; Keystone Varnish Company, printed litho label, 2.5" tall, $15. Radium Stove & Iron Enamel; J. L. Prescott Co., applied paper label, 8-ounce can, $10. Stein's Make-Up Grease Paint; The M. Stein Cosmetic Co., in box, $15. Motorkotor Auto Enamel; The Glidden Company, paper label, 1/2-pint can, $20.

E. E. Nice, "Fillers, Varnishes, Paints". Stoneware jug, $150.

Left to right: Rust-o-leum; Rust-o-leum, Inc., free sample, paper label, 2", $5. BPS Gloss Interior; The Patterson-Sargent Co., free sample, printed litho label, 2.25", $25. Sapolin Varnish Stains; Gerstendorfer Bros., free sample, paper label, 2" high, $35.

Wooden Shipping Boxes

Dutch Boy Flatting Oil. Hinged lid, $50.

Dutch Boy Flatting Oil. 5-gallon size, $50.

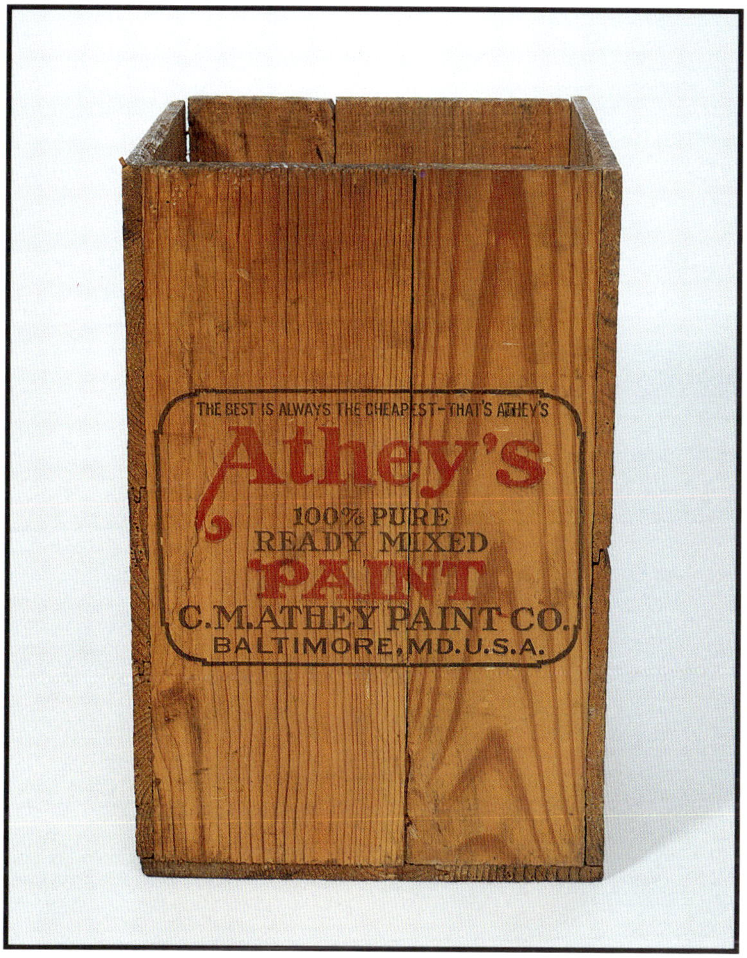

Athey Paint. Wooden box, $25.

Sherwin-Williams. Wooden box, $15.

BPS Paints. Wooden box, $35.

Arco Paints, Varnishes, and Enamels. Wooden box, $30.

BPS Paint. Barn paint, holds a 5-gallon can, applied paper label, $50.

Masury Ready Mixed Paints. Wooden box, $25.

Sherwin-Williams. Wooden box, $75.

The Martin-Senour Co., 100% Paints and Varnishes. Wooden box, $25.

Paint-Related Containers

Left: Cook Heavy Duty Maintenance Finishes, "Texaco" no. 14; Cook Paint and Varnish Company, quart can, $60. Right: International Premium Enamel; International Harvester, red, quart can, $50.

Left: Armstrong Paint & Varnish Thinner; Armstrong Paint & Varnish Works, paper label, cone top, $10. Right: Drake Paint & Varnish Thinner; Drake Paint Co., printed litho label, cone top, $25.

Chi-Namel Architectural Wood Finishes. The Ohio Varnish Co., 1/2-gallon can, $125.

Left to right: Brush-Nu Paint Brush Cleaner; 2 1/2-ounce cardboard container, $15. Rapid Paint Brush Cleaner, Mechling Bros. Chemicals, printed litho label, 3 ounce size, $10. Sample Perfection Paint Cleaner; printed litho label on top, $15. NuLife for paint brushes; Pittsburgh Plate Glass Company, printed litho label, pint can, $5. Savogran Paint Brush Cleaner; The Savogran Co., paper label, 4-ounce can, $10.

Left: Stein's Make-Up Grease Paint; The M. Stein Cosmetic Co., 1 5/8-ounce stick, makeup & box, $35. Makeup only, far right, $15. Center, Stein's Grease Paint Juvenile; The M. Stein Cosmetic Co., round tin, $20.

Left to right: Paint Brush Cleaner; Midway Chemical Co., 7-ounce can, printed litho label, $55. Savabrush; Schalk Chemical Company, printed litho label, 1/2-pound can, $55. Red Triangle Paint Brush Cleaner; Red Triangle Sales Co., printed litho label, 2 3/4-ounce can, $15.

Chapter Two

Paint Advertising

Metal Signs

Pittsburgh Paints "Smooth As Glass". Tin, flange, 30" x 25", excellent, $500.

Behr Process Paints and Finishes. Tin, single-sided, 22" x 18", NM, $150.

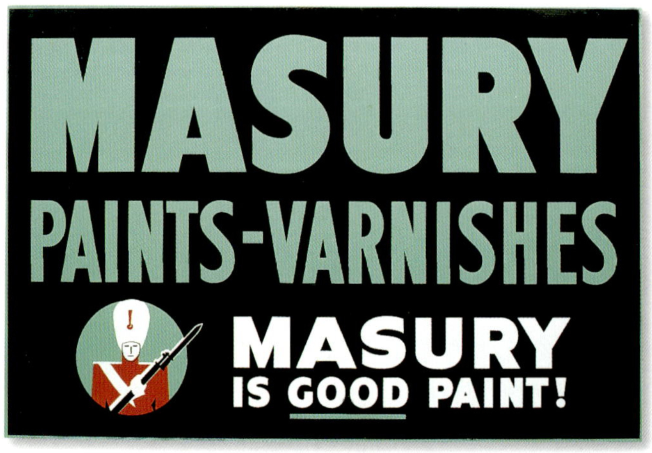

Masury Paints-Varnishes. Tin, flange, 36" x 24", NM, $400.

Mound City Paints. Embossed tin, single-sided, 27.25" x 19.75", exc., $550.

Chief Paints. Tin, double-sided, 28" x 12", NM, $100.

Acme Quality Paint. Enamel, double-sided, die-cut, 28" x 20", exc., $150.

Dutch Boy Paint, Dutch Boy on ladder. Tin, single-sided, 25.5" x 23.75", exc., $250.

Sherwin-Williams Paints and Varnishes. Porcelain, single-sided, 28" x 19.5", NM, $350.

Kurfees Paints, Enamels, Varnishes. Tin, single-sided, 20" x 14", exc., $100.

Devoe Paint and Varnish. Porcelain, flange, 18" x 14", NM, $200.

Lawrence Tiger Brand Paint. Porcelain, double-sided, 18" x 23", exc., $850.

Canada Paint. Porcelain, double-sided, 14" x 19", exc., $350.

Martin Senour Paints, Enamels, Varnishes. Tin, single-sided, 14" x 17", exc., $125.

Lowe Bros. Paints, L. L. Peavey Hardware. Porcelain, single-sided, 17.75" x 12", good, $95.

Davis Pure Paint Products. Porcelain, flange, 18" x 12", good, $150.

Condie-Bray Prepared Paint. Enamel, flange, 12" x 20", good, $325.

Keystone Paints. Porcelain, flange, 22" x 14", NM, $325.

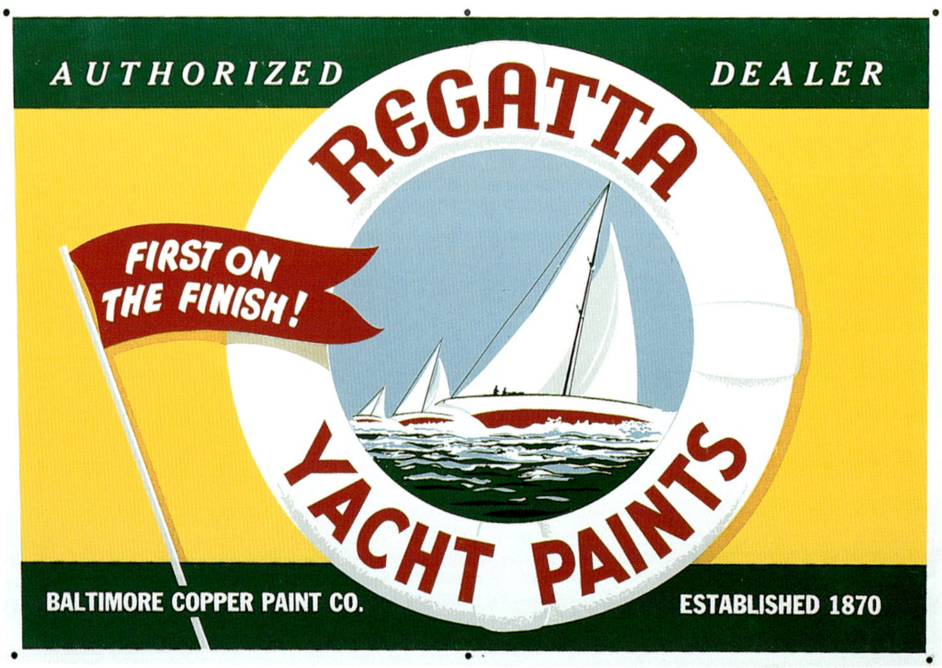

Regatta Yacht Paints. Tin, single-sided, 26" x 18", NM, $650.

Devoe Paints & Varnishes. Tin, flange, die-cut, 14" x 26", exc., $2225.

CIL Paints. Porcelain, double-sided, 24" x 18.5", NM, $275.

Vita-Var Paints. Enamel, flange, double-sided, 24" x 20", exc., $250.

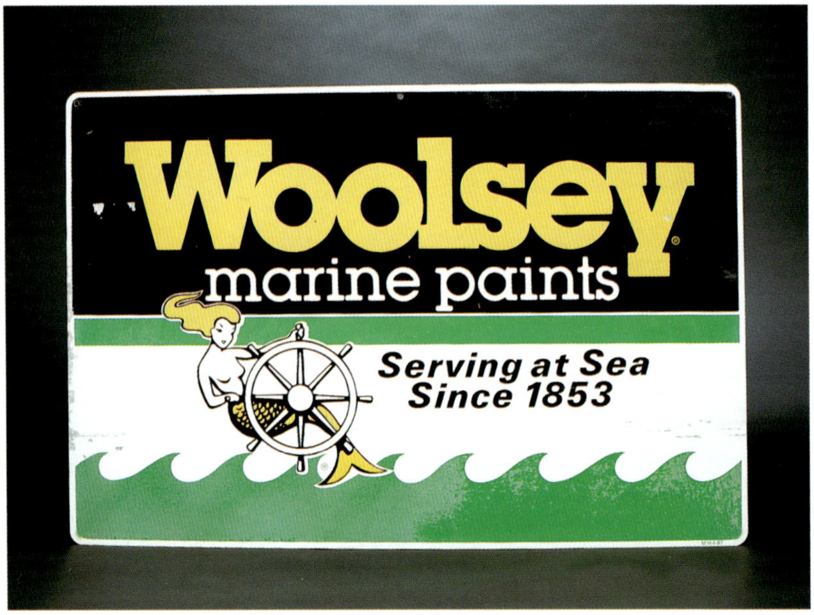

Woolsey Marine Paints. Tin, single-sided, 30" x 20", exc, $350.

Allied Paint. Porcelain, double-sided, 30" diameter, exc., $400.

Bay State Paint. Enamel, double-sided, 30" x 36", good, $225.

Du Pont Automobile Painting. Enamel, double-sided, 36" x 28", good, $275.

Breinig's Oil Paints. Wooden stencil, single-sided, 48" x 7.5", good, $100.

Heath & Milligan Paints & Varnishes. Metal rack sign, double-sided, 33" x 5", good, $150.

Lucas' Paint and Varnish. Thin tin, single-sided, 28" x 4.5", exc., $100.

Interlux Marine Finishes. Tin, self-framed, 56" x 32", exc., $2000.

Pabco Paints. Curved porcelain, single sided, 28" x 27.5", exc., $400.

Sherwin-Williams Paints, "Cover the Earth". Porcelain, flange, die-cut, 33.5" x 48", exc., $600.

BPS Paint Flatlux. Porcelain, double-sided, die-cut, 34" x 24", exc., $450.

Moore's House Paint. Tin, single-sided, die-cut, 35" x 23", exc., $150.

Sherwin-Williams Paints-Varnishes-Enamels. Curved porcelain, two single-sided back-to-back, 36" x 28", exc. $450.

BPS Best Paint. Porcelain, single-sided, 36" x 36", exc., $300.

A-M Paints. Tin, single-sided, die-cut, 27.5" x 58", good, $250.

Watertite Paints & Enamels. Tin, single-sided, 24" x 12", exc., $350.

Martin Senour Colors in Paint. Tin, flange, die-cut, 19" x 18" exc., $425.

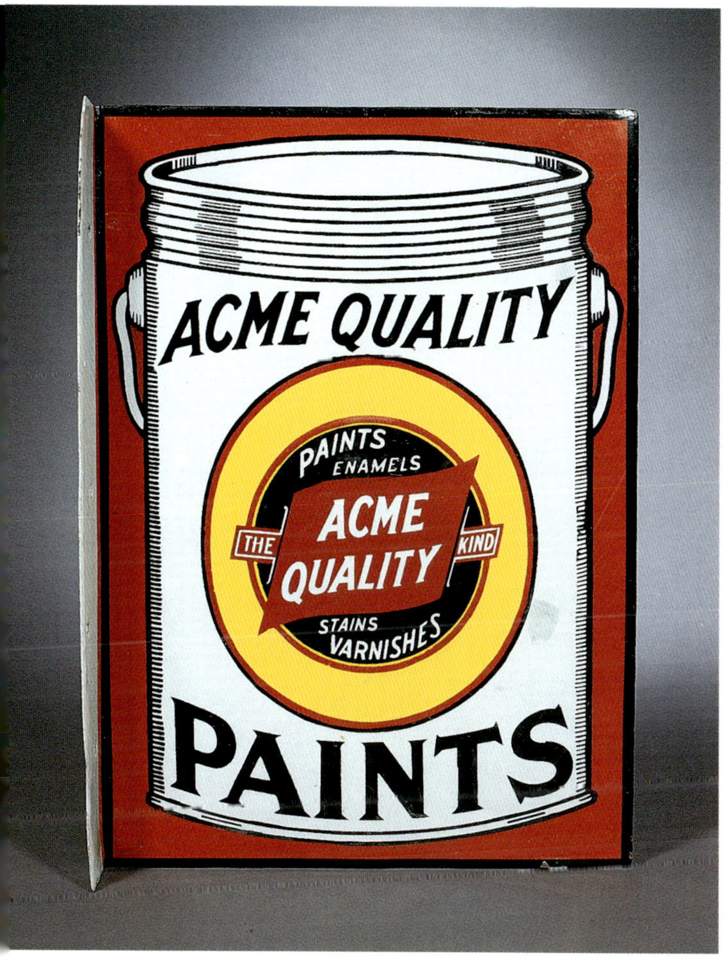

Acme Quality Paints. Porcelain, flange, 14.5" x 20", exc., $425.

Davis Pure Paint Products. Porcelain, flange, 18" x 13", exc., $425.

Sapolin Paints. Enamel, double-sided, 44" x 22", exc., $325.

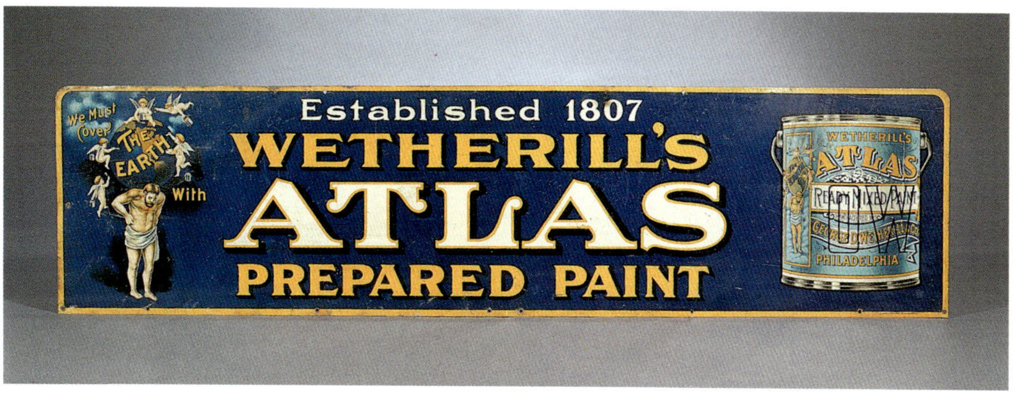

Wetherill's Atlas Prepared Paint. Tin, single-sided, 40" x 10", exc., $350.

Canada Paint Co. C & P House Paint and Luxor Supreme Enamel.
Double-sided, flange, 14" x 18", exc. $275.

Sherwin-Williams Paints. Porcelain, double-sided, hanging, die-cut, 24" x 10.5", good, $375.

BPS "Free Sample Can". Tin, single-sided, exc., $250.

Armor Coat Paint. Porcelain, double-sided, 24" x 48", exc., $800.

Burdsal's Paints. Porcelain, double-sided, 16.5" x 30", exc., $600.

BPS "Look Into It". Porcelain, flange, 14" x 20", good, $350.

Masury Paint Store. Porcelain, flange, 24" x 16", exc., $400.

Billings-Chapin Paints. Porcelain, double-sided, 24" x 21.5", NM, $1500.

Martin-Senour Monarch Paint. Porcelain, flange, 17" x 15.5", exc., $400.

H. S. Lowe Brothers. Porcelain, single-sided, 24" x 17", good, $250.

Chi-Namel Paints. Porcelain, double-sided, bracket, 9.5" x 30" (w/o bracket), exc., $600.

Pittsburgh Sun-Proof Paint. Tin, self-framed, 36" x 25.5", exc., $425.

Lowe Brothers Paints. Tin, single-sided, 36" x 18", exc., $250.

Dutch Boy Paints. Porcelain, double-sided, die-cut, 54.5" x 30", exc., $800.

Ramsay's Paints. Porcelain, double-sided, 24" x 19", exc., $300.

Edward Smith's Marine Paints and Varnishes. Porcelain, single-sided, 29.5" x 12", exc., $250.

Dutch Boy. Tin, self-framed, 34.5" x 23", exc., $200.

Light-Ups & Glass

Klimate-Pruf Paints. Glass reverse painted, 16" x 8", NM., $250.

McQuade Paints. Glass reverse painted, 20" x 10", exc., $150.

Sargent Paint Products. The Sargent Gerke Co., light-up counter display sign, 13" wide x 17" high, exc., $200.

Lucas, "a Great Name in Paints". Embossed plastic face with inside light, chain and metal easel, exc., $75.

Duco Du Pont. Oval red neon, 12" x 5", exc., $250.

Dutch Boy. Can-shaped plastic face with plastic top and base, inside light, 12" x 16", exc., $200

Gallery Paint Company. Lamp, 16" tall, 1985, $35.

COLOR CHARTS

Kwickwork Auto Enamels. Wooden half-wheel with spokes as colors of enamels, 24.5", $650.

Lucas Carriage Gloss Paint. John Lucas & Co., celluloid sign (frame not original), 9" x 13", $350.

Valentine's Valspar Varnish Stain. Valentine & Company, celluloid over cardboard, easel back with rope, 11" x 14", $150.

Chi-Namel Rapido Enamels. Tin with wooden paint color samples, 26" x 13", missing four samples, $150; complete, $300.

Sargent Floor and Furniture Enamel. The Sargent-Gerke Co., floor-standing color display (missing paint color inserts), 23" x 27". As is, $100; complete, $250.

Sargent Floor and Furniture Enamel. The Sargent-Gerke Co., counter display, $150.

Kyanize Sanitary Floor Enamel. Celluloid over tin, easel back with chain for hanging, Patented Dec.18, 1900, 11" x 17", $250.

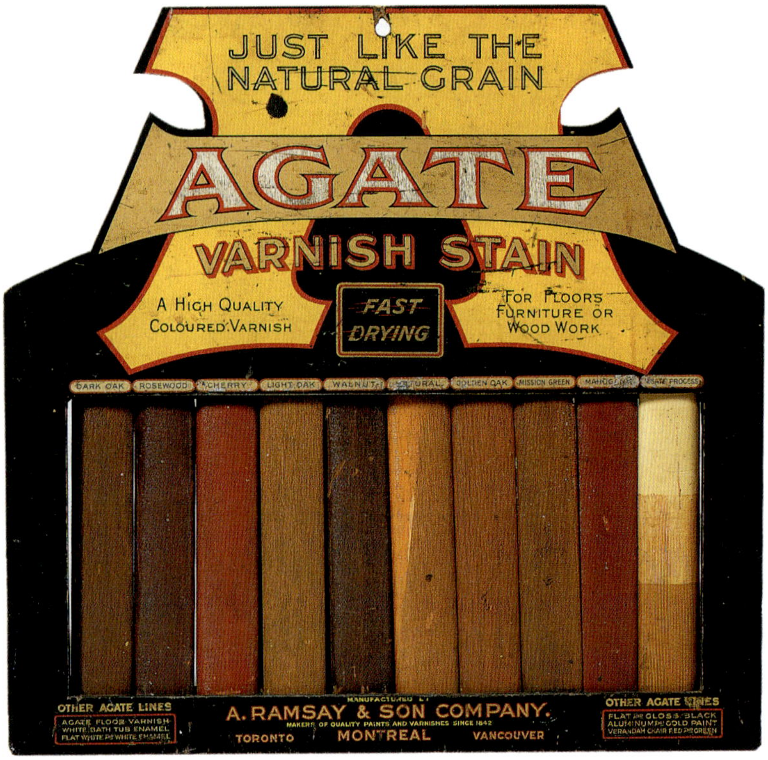

Agate Varnish Stain. Wooden, easel/hanging, individual wooden paint color samples, exc., $65.

Regatta Yacht Paint. Baltimore Copper Paint Co., celluloid over cardboard, easel back with chain for hanging, 13" x 20.75", $100.

Sani-Flat. Benjamin Moore & Company, Ltd, wooden frame with wooden paint color samples, exc., $75.

Carmote Enamel. Counter color display with inserts, 27" x 12", $75.

Lowe Brothers High Standard Liquid Paint. Wire easel back, tin with removable wooden paint samples, 8.5" x 16", $175.

Sun-Proof House Paint. Pittsburgh Plate Glass Company, tin with wooden removable paint samples, 4.5" x 25", $100.

New England's Best Flat Wall Paint. New England Oil Paint & Varnish Co., easel back, heavy cardboard with string hanger, 15.5" x 19.75", $100.

Left: Bru-Lux Enamel; Bruning Brothers, celluloid over cardboard, 6" x 20" wide, $50. Right: SWP House Paint; Sherwin-Williams, paper on masonite, 5" x 18", $50.

Left: Valon Flat Wall Paint; Valspar, celluloid over cardboard, 5" x 20", $15. Right: Valspar Semi-Gloss For Walls and Woodwork; celluloid over cardboard, 5" x 20", $15.

Left to right: Warren's Floor Enamel; Warren Paint & Color Co., celluloid over tin, easel back and chain for hanging, patented Nov. 10, 1914, 6.5" x 6", $35. D & B Paint Products; The Dean & Barry Co., celluloid over tin, 7" x 15", $75. Comet Quick Dry Enamel; celluloid over cardboard, 4.5" x 10.25", $65. Sargent Enamel for Truck and Tractor; The Sargent-Gerke Co., celluloid over tin, 4" x 10.5", $75.

BPS Items, left to right: "FloorWay", paint brush (missing handle) $175; celluloid button, 2" diameter, $40; "Best Paint Sold", color card holder, $225.

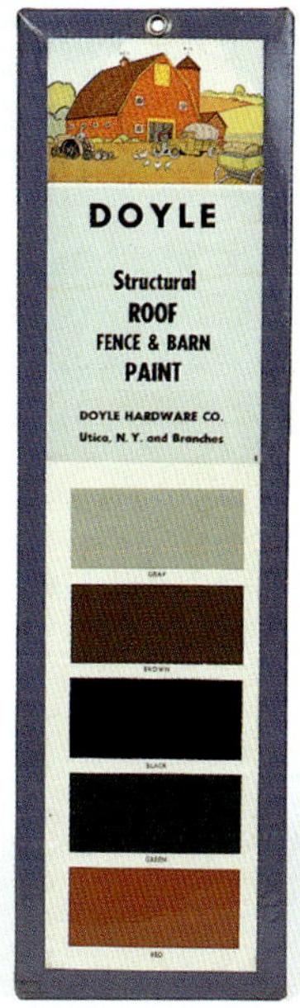

Doyle Roof, Fence and Barn Paint. Celluloid over cardboard, 4.5" x 15.5", $50.

Left: Davis "On the face of things", color card holder, $325. Right: Lucas "Paints & Varnishes", color card holder, $375.

Left: National Lead Co., hinged aluminum case with color cards, 2.25" x 3.25", $75.
Right: Martin Senour, "Kolor Brite" fan-type paint chart in folder, $20.

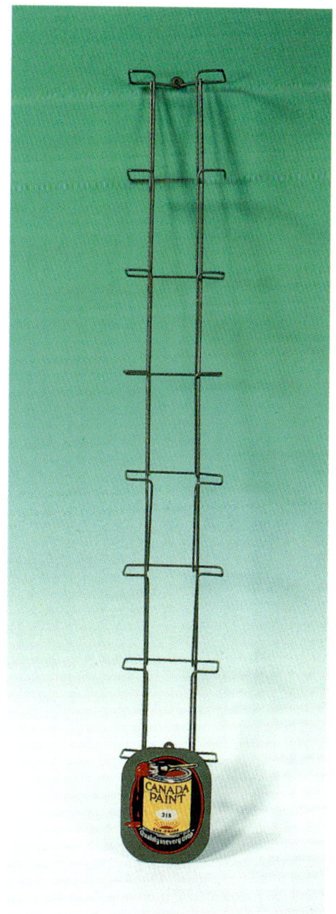

Canada Paint, hanging paint chart rack, exc., 4" x 32", $100.

Clocks

Hansen Hardware, Authorized Dealer Janney Best Paints. Plastic advertising face, metal frame, paint cans around clock face, $325.

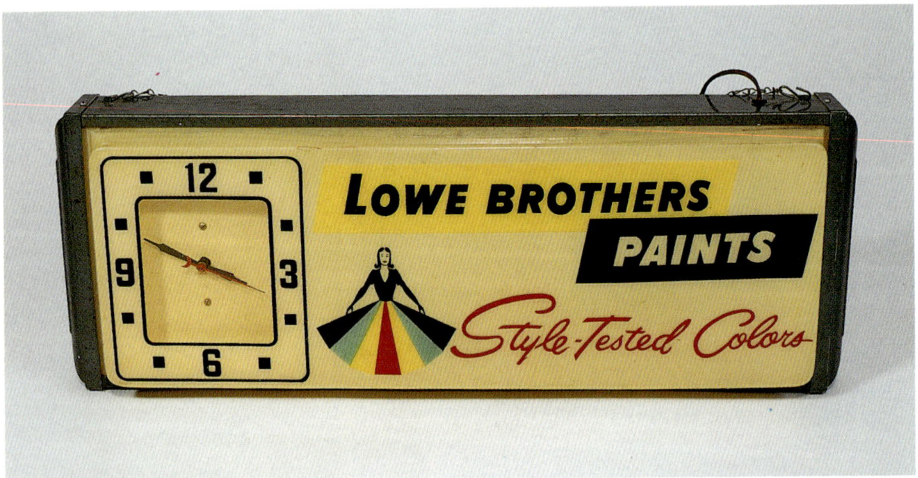

Lowe Brothers Paints. Plastic pan face, $175.

Sherwin-Williams Paints. Plastic face with metal frame, $150.

Wetherill's Atlas Paints. Octagon neon spinner, $600.

Seidlitz Multi Tint Paints. Numbers cut out so light comes through, bubble face, $800.

Kurfees Paint, double bubble, $700.

Du Pont Duco Dulex. Pam-style clock, $400.

Du Pont Dulux Yacht Finishes. Pam-style clock, $400.

Allentown Paints. Pam clock, $300.

Athey's Paints. Plastic light-up, $150.

Paragon Paints, $150.

Eaglo. Large Pam, 1964, $350.

THERMOMETERS

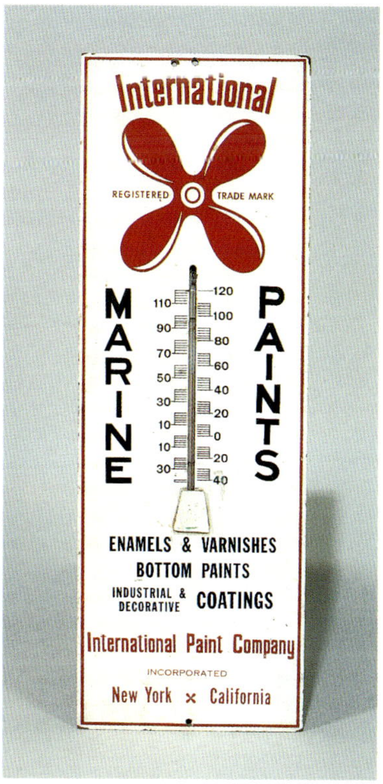

International Marine Paints. International Paint Company, masonite, 20", $150.

Kuhn's Climatized Paint, enamel, 38", $300.

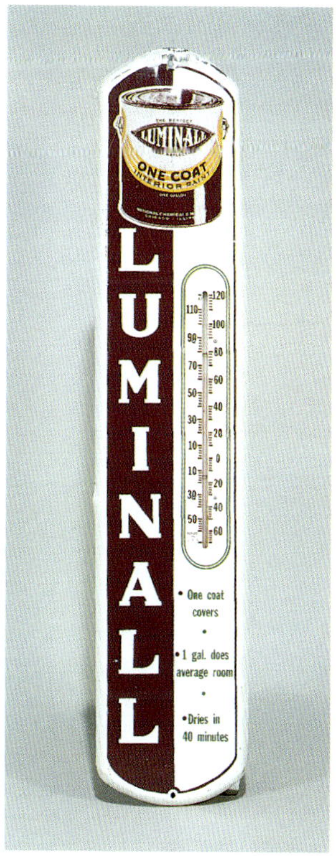

Luminall, "One Coat Interior Paint". Tin, 38", $125.

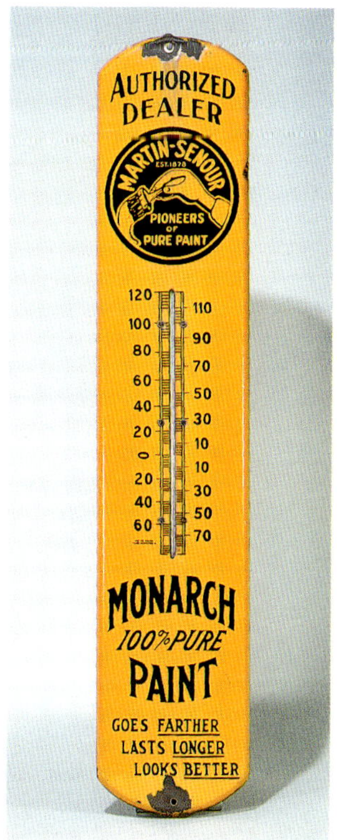

Martin-Senour Monarch. Porcelain, 38", $255.

Luxor. The Canada Paint Co. Limited, porcelain, 30", $550.

Interlux. International Paint Company, 12" Pam, $225.

Gray-Seal Paint, 12" diameter, $125.

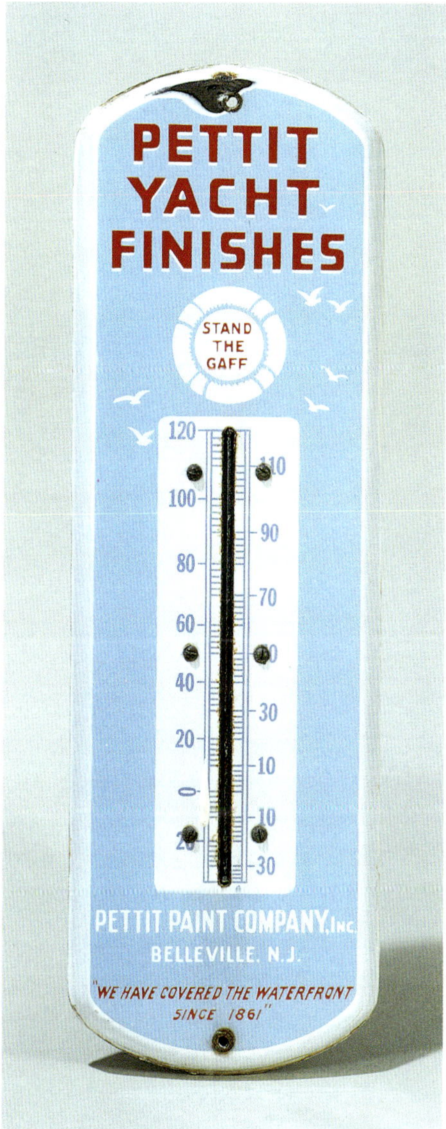

Pettit Yacht Finishes. Pettit Paint Company, Inc., porcelain, 19", $275.

Ditzler Automotive Finishes, 12" diameter, $100.

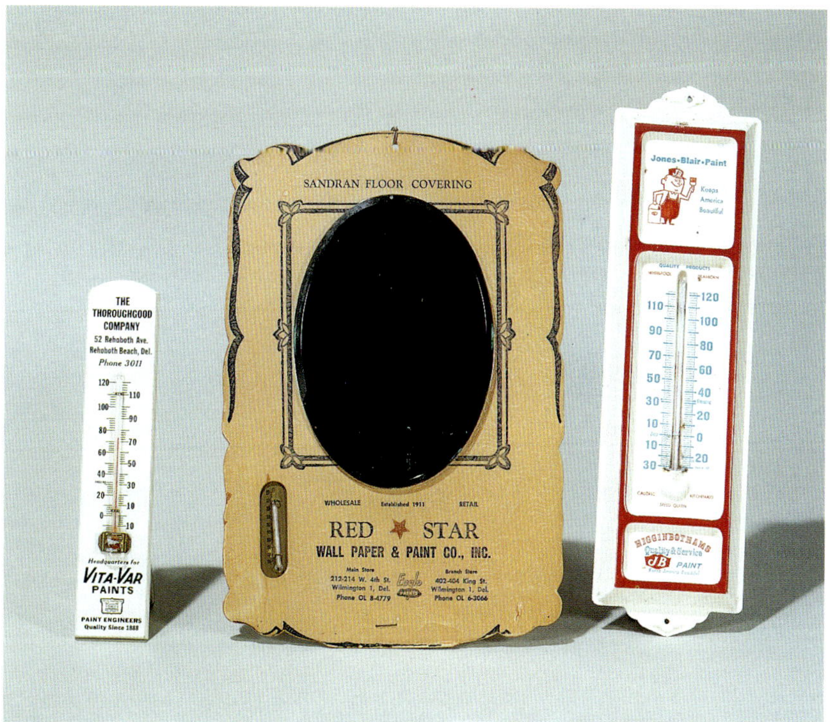

Left to right: Vita-Bar Paints, wooden, 8", $45. Red Star Wall Paper & Paint Co. Inc., cardboard with mirror, 12", $75. Jones-Blair Paint, painted tin, 13", $25.

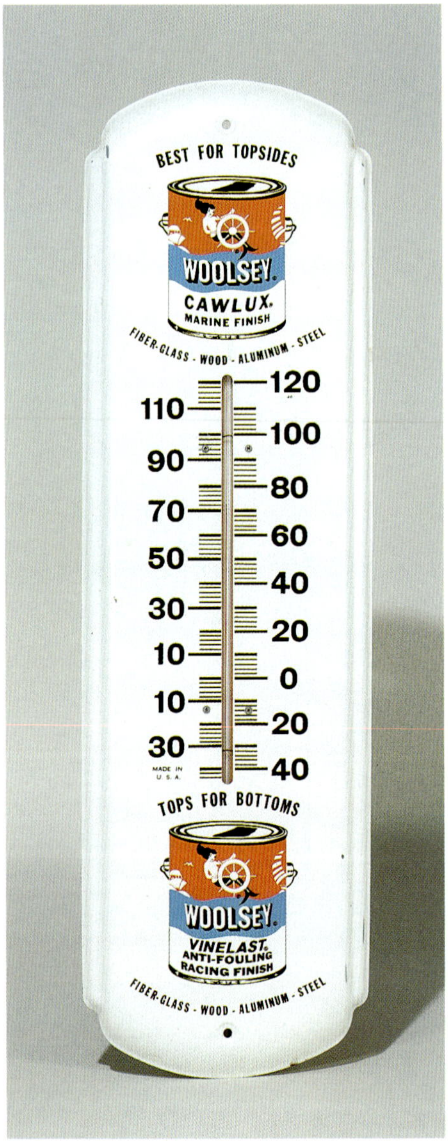

Woolsey Cawlux Marine Finish. Tin, 27", $225.

Martin-Senour Paints. Tin, 28", $75.

Ox-Line Paints. Ox-line Paint Company, 12" diameter, $175.

Carter White Lead Paint. Porcelain, 27", $325.

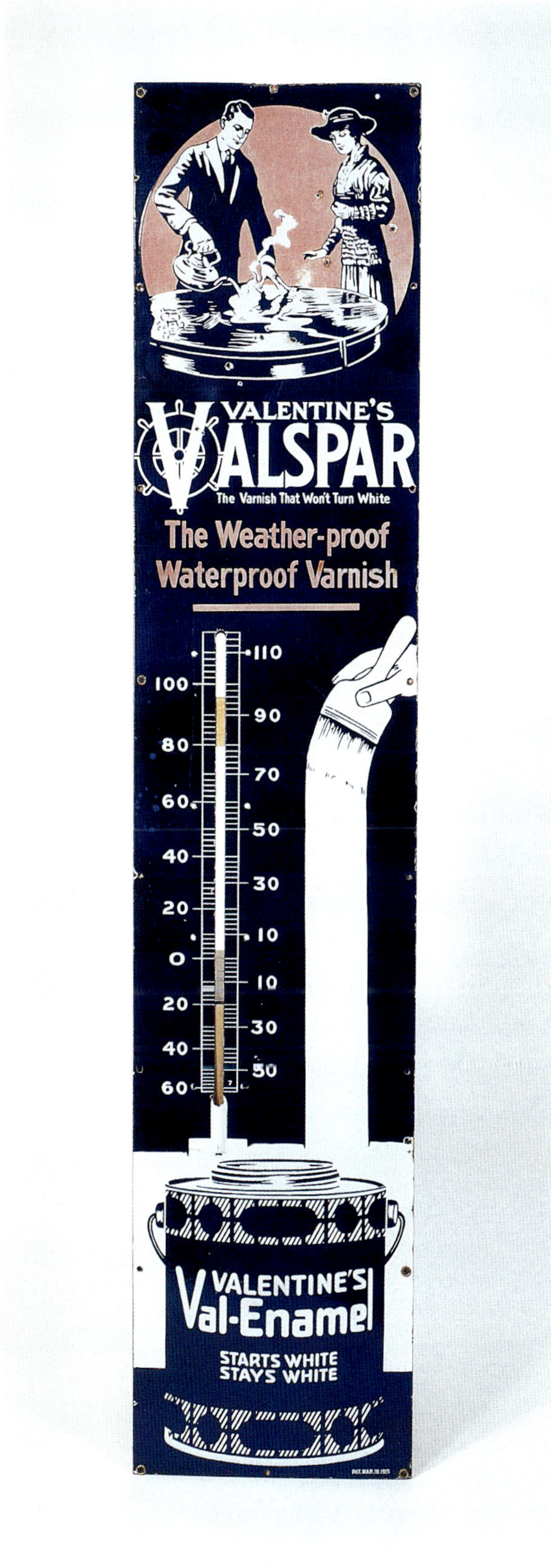

Valentine's Valspar Val-Enamel. Porcelain, tube missing, 15" x 71", $950.

Chapter Three

Paint Store Displays & Painter Supplies

Store Displays

Sherwin-Williams Paints. Wooden hanging cabinet—circa 1900s—for paint and brushes. Note the chameleon design on the door. 19" x 28", exc., $900.

Dutch Boy. Pressed cardboard figure, 29", exc., $750.

Dutch Boy. Pressed cardboard figure with cardboard sign, 23" including pole, NM, $400.

Benjamin Moore, "Time To Paint" cardboard display, 13" x 9.5", NM, $100.

Dutch Boy. Ceramic lamp, 21.5" tall, exc, $175.

Dutch Boy Paints. Molded rubber Dutch Boy on top of paint can with wooden base, 20.5" tall, exc., $500.

DuLux Du Pont. Shelving unit for paint, 30" x 32", exc., $150.

Martin-Senour Paint. Display for paint cans, 8" x 13", exc., $250.

Murphy's Quick Velvet Enamel, display for paint jars, 13" x 12", exc., $150.

Ford Color Patch. Display with 15 cans of touch-up paint, 12" x 18.5", NM, $650.

Sapolin Gold Enamel. Picture of George Washington mounted in a gold frame and wooden shadow box, easel, 10" x 14", NM, $600.

BPS House Paint. Man behind counter, dated 1924, cardboard, easel back, 34.5" x 29.5", exc., $350.

BPS Floor and Deck Enamel. Can topper, cardboard, exc., $75.

BPS cardboard sign, double-sided, could have fit in frame, 31" x 20.75", NM, $95.

Crown Diamond Tops. Cardboard, easel back, exc., $125.

Free Can of BPS for You! Easel back, die-cut cardboard, 21" x 28", NM, $125.

BPS cardboard sign, double-sided, could have fit in frame, 31" x 20.75", NM, $95.

BPS House Paint, easel backs, cardboard, exc., 10" tall, $75 each.

Zan-Z-Lac. Davis Paint Co., has been framed, paper, 18" x 28" before frame, exc., $300.

Dinah Black Enamel. Easel back, die-cut cardboard, 20" x 25", mint, $550.

Dinah Black Enamel. Display has woman holding real can of paint. Easel back, die-cut cardboard, 12" x 14", mint, $350.

Devoe 2-Coat System. Easel back, die-cut cardboard, 26" x 39", NM, $150.

Du Pont Paints. Easel back, 3D, die-cut cardboard, 21.5" x 53", exc., $750.

Du Pont Duco. Easel back, die-cut cardboard, 20" x 30", exc., $125.

Du Pont. Easel back, 3D, die-cut cardboard, framed, 23" x 41.5", NM, $600.

Du Pont Duco. Easel back, die cut cardboard, 12" x 18", NM, $150.

Du Pont Duco. Easel back, die cut cardboard, 12" x 18", exc., $100.

Du Pont Duco. Cardboard, easel back, has been framed, 9.75" x 19.75", NM, $150.

Du Pont Duco, Walt Disney Productions, cardboard, easel back, 29" x 40", exc., $325.

Du Pont Bridgeport Standard. Easel back (has been framed), 3-D, die-cut cardboard, 21" x 43" before framing, exc., $750.

Dutch Boy, Paint News. Easel back, die-cut cardboard, 16.25" x 32.75", exc., $475.

Dutch Boy. Easel back, die-cut cardboard, 11.75", NM, $75.

Dutch Boy White Lead. Easel back, 2-piece, 3-D, die-cut cardboard, exc., $450.

Dutch Boy Soft Paste. 3-D foldout, die-cut cardboard, approx. size of each piece 17.5" x 14". Could be part of set, NM, $125 each.

Dutch Boy White Lead Window Display. Two main sections are 3-D, foldout, die-cut cardboard, easel back. Individual small Dutch Boy figures, which are foldouts, would be placed in front of main sections. 1930s, NM, $1500.

Dutch Boy. Easel back, die-cut cardboard, 11" x 20", NM, $175 each.

Dutch Boy. Can topper, die-cut cardboard, 8.5" tall, NM, $75 each.

Dutch Boy. Masonite stand-up figure, 57.5" tall, $150.

Dutch Boy Paints for Double Duty. Easel back, 3-D, die-cut cardboard, 46" x 29", exc., $150.

Dutch Boy Quick-Drying Enamel. 3-D, easel back, cardboard, 19" x 29", exc., $350.

Dutch Boy White Lead, holding kite string (may have had a kite), easel back, cardboard, 20" x 31", NM, $350.

Dutch Boy, double-sided, die-cut cardboard with holes for hanging, 9" x 11", NM, $150 each.

Dutch Boy, "Paint Outside with Dutch Boy White Lead". Easel back, die-cut cardboard, 10" x 12", Exc., $175.

Dutch Boy. Easel back, 3-D, die-cut cardboard, 44" x 43", Exc., $500.

Dutch Boy, small individual boys approx. 10" tall with hole under arm, single-sided, cardboard, NM, $75 each.

Dutch Boy. Easel back, 3-D, die-cut cardboard, 32" x 46", 1920s, NM, $850.

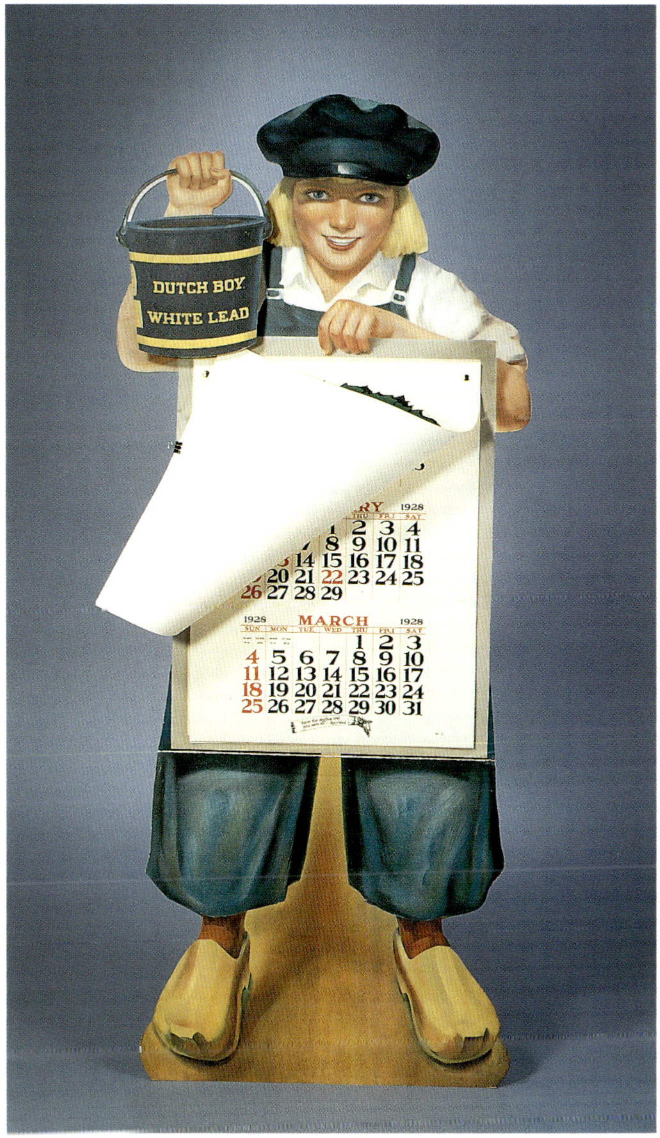

Dutch Boy. Easel back, 3-D, die-cut cardboard, unused 1928 calendar, cover page has Christmas wreath, 21.5" x 51.5", mint, $875.

Dutch Boy. Easel back, 3-D, die-cut cardboard, part of another display, 34.5" x 31.5", NM, $450.

Dutch Boy. Easel back, 3-D, die-cut cardboard, NRA logo bottom left, 32" x 36", exc., $800.

Dutch Boy. Double-sided, die-cut cardboard with holes for hanging, 10.5" x 18" each, NM, $225 each.

Dutch Boy. Self-framed cardboard, 22" x 32", good, $250.

Glidden. Cardboard over tin, dated May 14, 1918, 42" x 30", exc., $250.

GP Undercoat. Flat cardboard, 14.5" x 19", NM, $75.

Kem-Glo and Kem-Tone. Flat double-sided cardboard, both sides shown, 35" x 30", exc., $75.

Kem-Glo and Kem-Tone. Flat double-sided cardboard, both sides shown, 35" x 30", $75.

Kem-Tone lady standup. 36" x 66", 3-D, real clothes, with promotional easel back cardboard, mint, $100.

Lowe Brothers, "Paint for Health". 3-D foldout display, cardboard, 66" x 36", one piece missing, exc., $125.

Kem-Tone lady. Easel back, cardboard, 22" x 60", mint, $200.

Lowe Brothers, "Sparkling Color". 3-D foldout, card-board, 23.5" x 34", exc., $100.

Lowe Brothers Floor Paint. Easel back, cardboard, 24.25" x 30", exc., $250.

Lucas Durafilm. 3-D foldout, cardboard, 13" x 15.5", exc., $150.

Lucas Quick Drying Enamels. Easel back, die-cut cardboard, 20" x 14", exc., $100.

Lucas—Paints for the Entire House. Cardboard mobile, NM, $150.

Mautz Paint. Cardboard easel-back painter figures, exc.; large (15") $100 each; small (9") $75 each.

Lucas Household Enamel. Flat cardboard, exc., $100.

Martin-Senour Paint. "If it's worth covering...", paper sign, 40.5" x 22", exc., $250.

Benjamin Moore Paint. Cardboard window display set, easel back, 3-D, includes pieces for paint cans, mint, $200.

O'Brien's Flexico. Easel back, cardboard, 20" x 28", exc., $125.

New Jersey Mixed Paints. Wax cardboard sign, 13.75" x 13.75", exc., $35.

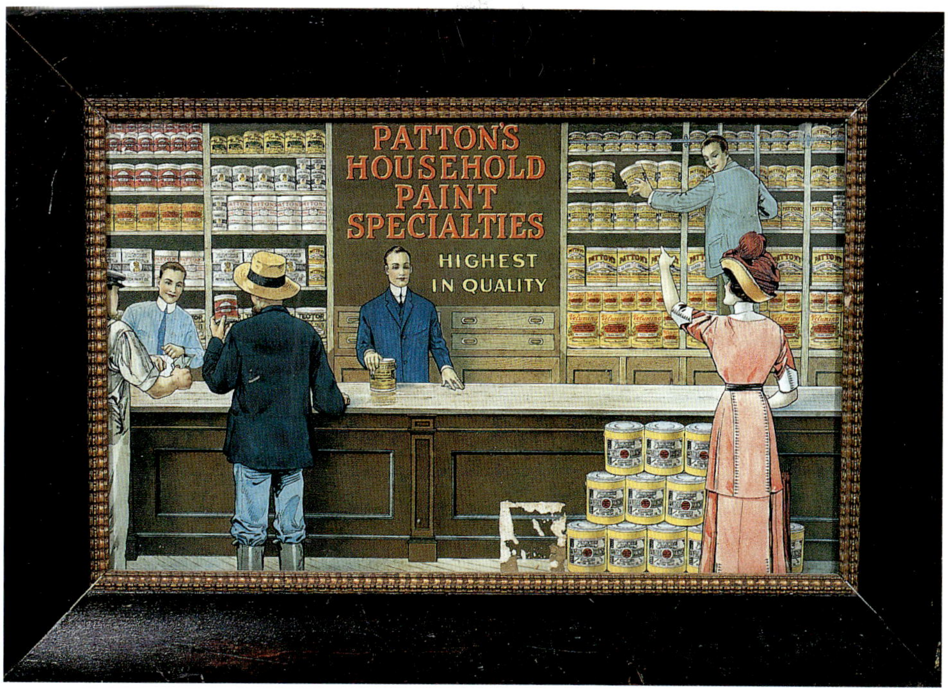

Patton's Household Paint Specialities. Paper sign (frame added), exc., $325.

Quality American Seal Ready Mixed Paint, Uncle Sam & Miss Liberty. Easel back, die cut cardboard, two pieces, 16.75" x 48" each, exc., $1500 for pair.

Pierce's Paints-Varnishes. Cardboard sign, die cut, 21" x 32.5", exc., $250.

Pittsburgh Paints, Sun-Proof. Easel back, die-cut cardboard, 3-D, 28" x 39.5", NM, $175.

Pittsburgh Paint. Easel back, die-cut cardboard, 3-D, 21" x 53", exc., $550.

Pratt & Lambert Paint and Varnish. Lighthouse design, cardboard, easel back, 28" x 38", NM, $200.

Rogers Paint Lasts. Easel back, die-cut cardboard, 26.25" x 43", NM, $200.

Rogers House Paint, “Blackstone the famous Magician”. Easel back, die-cut cardboard, 27.5" x 43.5", NM, $675.

Rogers Paint Lasts, easel back, die cut cardboard, 26.25" x 43", NM. $200.

Sapolin Stove Pipe Enamel. Easel back, cardboard, 6.5" x 8", NM, $225.

Sapolin Stove Pipe Enamel. Easel back, cardboard, 35.5" x 33.5", exc., $475.

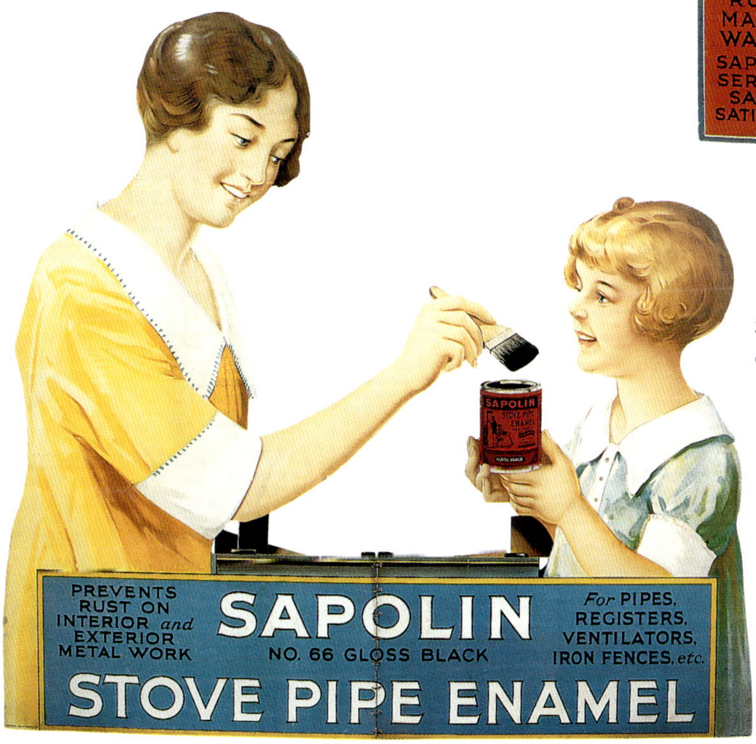

Sapolin Stove Pipe Enamel. Easel back, cardboard, 32" x 33", exc., $475.

Sapolin Stove Pipe Enamel. Easel back, cardboard, 32" x 32", exc., $475.

Sherwin-Williams. Three-piece cardboard easel-back display, middle section 18" x 27", missing pieces, NM, $125.

Sherwin-Williams Enameloid. Two pieces, cardboard, parts missing, no easel, 24.75" x 36.75", NM, $125.

Sherwin-Williams. Easel back, die-cut cardboard, 12" x 16" each, NM, $250 pr.

Sherwin-Williams. Flat double-sided cardboard, both sides shown, 35" x 30", exc., $75.

Sherwin-Williams. Flat double-sided cardboard, both sides shown, 24" x 18.5", exc., $75.

SWP, The Sherwin-Williams Co. Cardboard, easel backs, 15" x 20", exc. $100; good $50.

SWP, The Sherwin-Williams Co. Cardboard, easel back, 15" x 20", exc., $125.

Sherwin-Williams Kem-1-Coat. 3-D paint can, heavy paper, 18" diameter x 21" high, mint, $100.

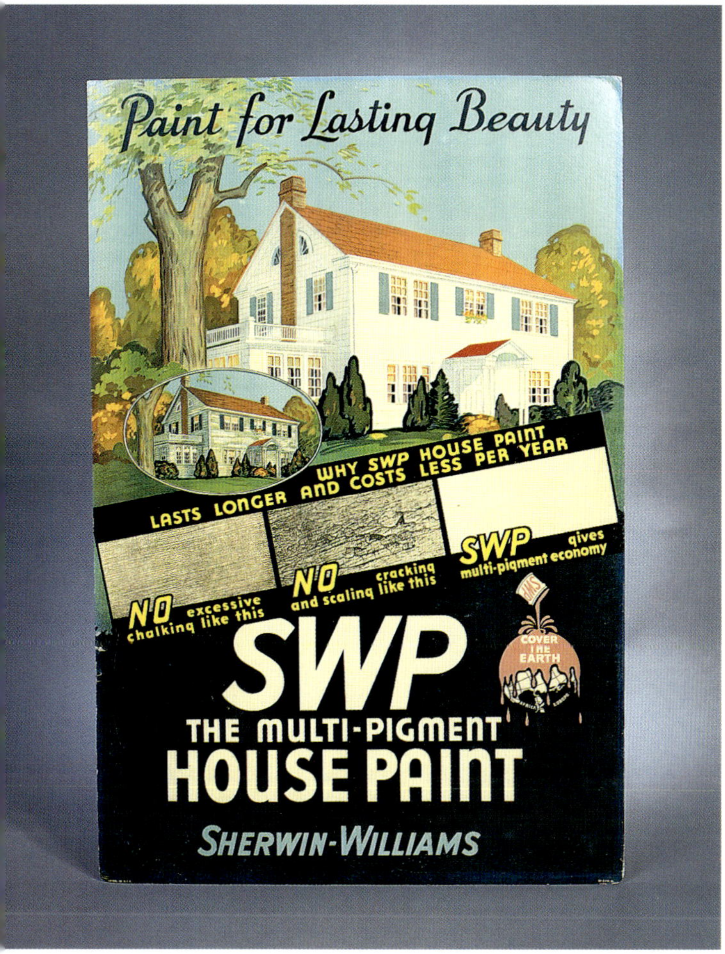

"Paint Now With Sherwin-Williams". Paper, die-cut, 19" x 16", exc., $75.

Sherwin-Williams, SWP House Paint. flat cardboard, 25" x 37", NM, $100.

Sherwin-Williams, SWP House Paint. Easel back, die-cut cardboard, 29.5" x 27", NM, $160.

Sherwin-Williams, Flat-Tone. Cardboard, easel back, 3-piece display, main section 25" x 37", NM, $200.

Sherwin-Williams House Paint Lasts Longer. Cardboard, easel back, 22" x 60", mint, $200.

Sherwin-Williams. Cardboard, easel backs, dated 1940, NM, larger (18" x 11.5") $100 each; smaller $50.

SWP Sherwin-Williams House Paint. Cardboard, easel-back 3-D foldout, die-cut, 39" x 29", NM, $425.

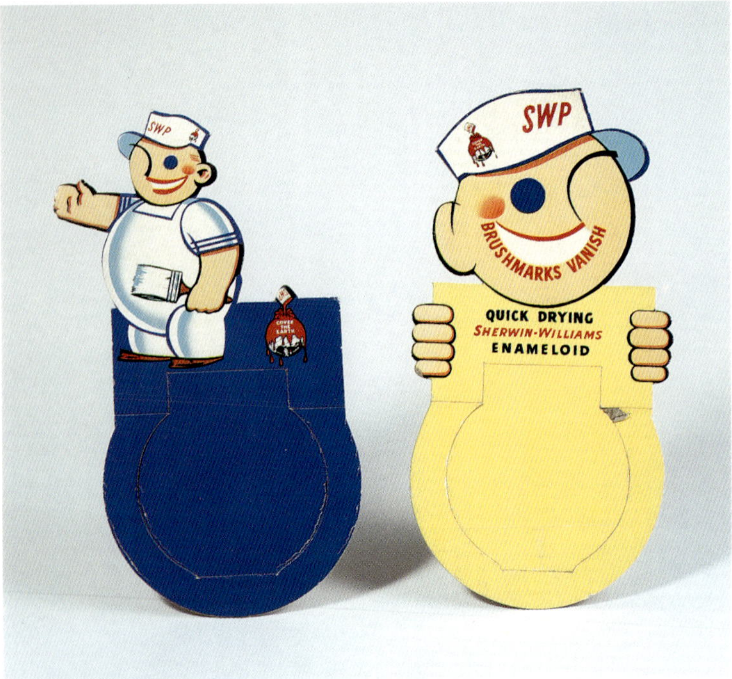

SWP paint can toppers. 12" tall, exc., each $75.

Siscolin Washable Distemper. Cardboard, easel back, 18.5" x 29", good, $250.

Warren's Insured Paint. Easel back, die-cut cardboard, 9" x 18", exc., $225.

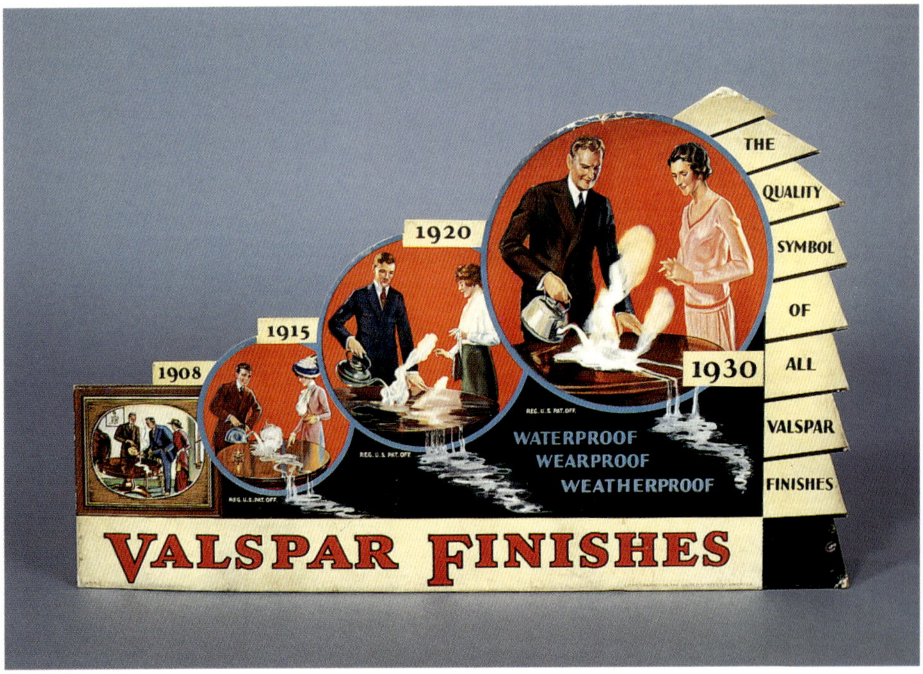

Valspar Finishes. Easel back, die-cut cardboard, 19" x 11.5", exc., $100.

Calendars

Dutch Boy Calendars, 9" x 16" (left to right): "Tom Sawyer Boss Painter", 1923, full pad, $175; "The Dutch Boy Painter", 1922, full pad, $150; "Joan", signed Haskell Coffin, 1922, full pad, $175.

Atlantic White Lead "The Dutch Boy Painter". 1915 calendar missing, however, 1916 calendar is printed on the canvas cloth material. 15" x 38.5", $300.

Charles A. Collier—Painter, Decorator, Paper Hanger. Cardboard hanging (has been framed), 1902, 12" x 15", $175.

Lucas Paints, John Lucas & Co., The Signing of the Declaration of Independence. 1908 paper hanging (shown in frame), 14" x 24", $150.

Rubber Paint Co. Postcard size, back side is 1886 calendar, $20.

Campbell Glass & Paint Co. 1912 calendar, postcard size, $20.

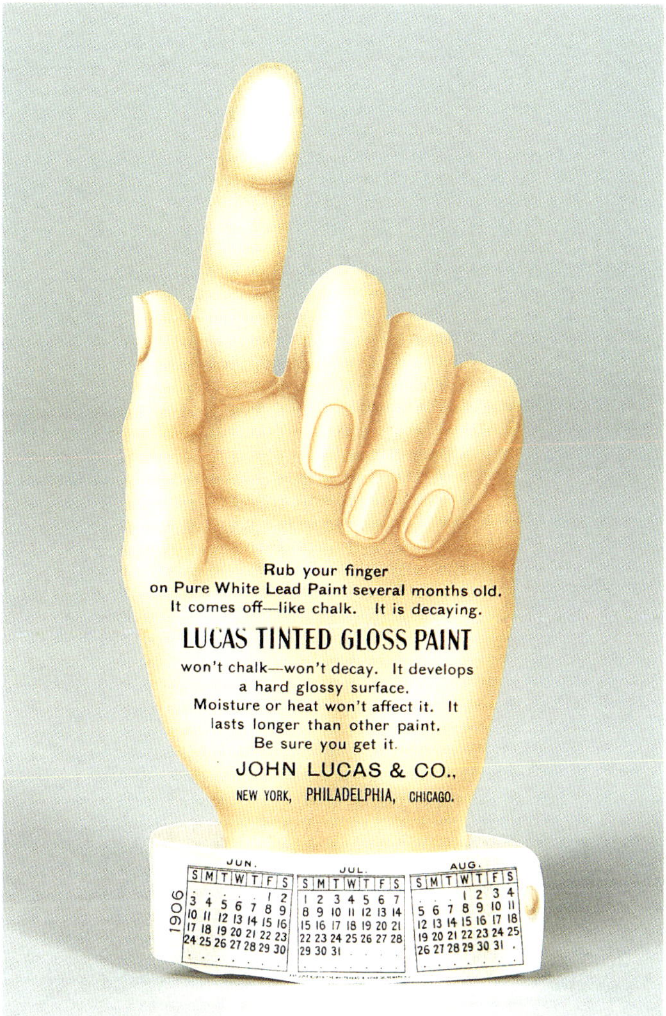

Lucas Tinted Gloss Paint. John Lucas & Co., 1906, die-cut celluloid, 2.25" x 5.25", $275.

Sherwin-Williams Paint, calendar and full-color paint samples, postcard size, 1901, $40.

Dutch Boy Christmas Calendar, 1950. When opened, it shows miscellaneous photos, months and name of merchant, exc., $25.

Wet Paint Signs

Clockwise from left: Eagle White Lead, $20 each; Lawrence Paint Varnish, $30.

Benjamin Moore & Co. Top $20, middle $15; bottom $15.

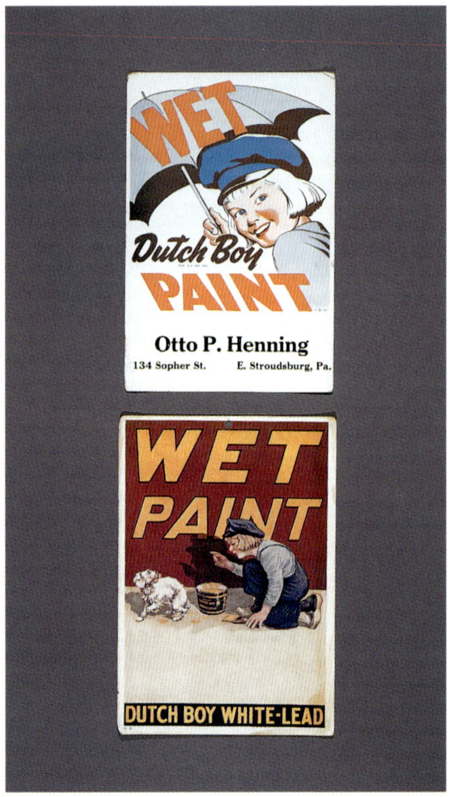

Dutch Boy Paint. Top $25; bottom $20.

Clockwise from left: Wetherill & Brother, $15; MAB, $25; Benjamin Moore & Co., $20.

Dutch Boy Paint, each $20.

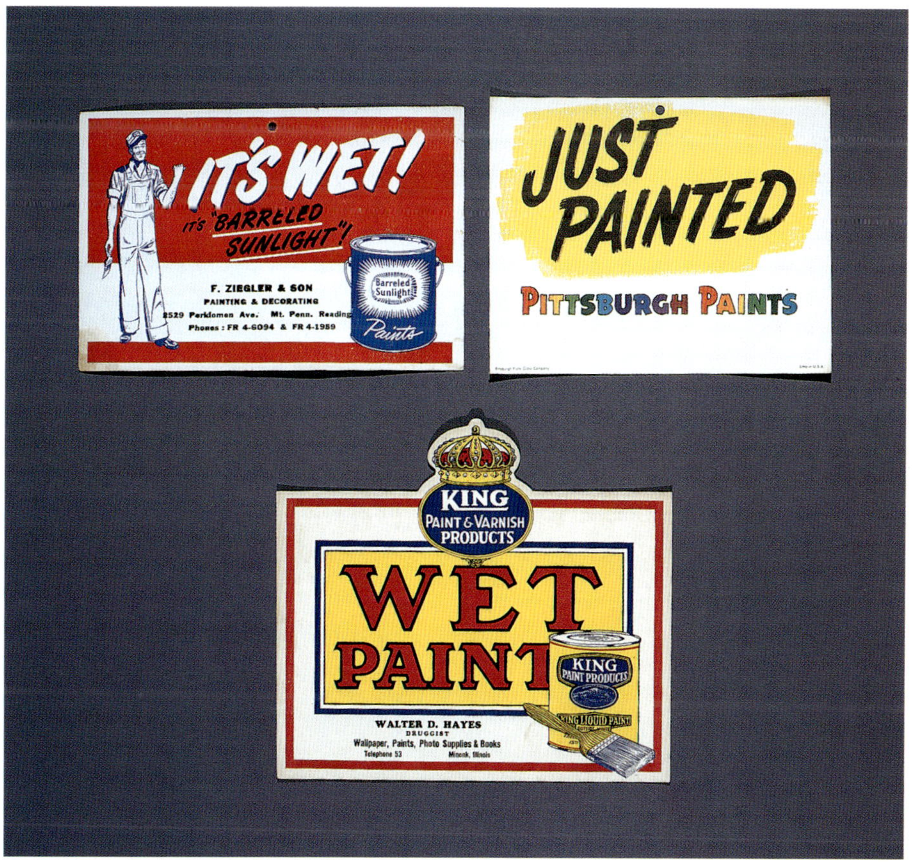

Clockwise from left: Barreled Sunlight, $20; Pittsburgh Paints, $15; King Paint Products, $30.

Clockwise from top: Lewis White Lead, $25; Chi-Namel, $35; Dutch Boy, $20.

Mautz, large paper wet paint sign, $15.

Stephens' Paint, $20;
Sherwin-Williams, $30.

Clockwise from left: Devoe Paint, $20; Enterprise Paint, $15; Du Pont, $20.

Paper Items

Dutch Boy Painter Magazines. Includes information about Dutch Boy products and shows some wonderful early window displays. These were given to house painters to show them how to paint, tips of the trade and how to run a painting business. $8 each.

Top row: Montgomery Ward & Co. Paint Catalogue. Special issue with 33 pages covering all the brands of their paint, as well as color chips of each type of paint. Also covered are brushes, ladders, wallpaper designs, almost everything you would need to order for remodelling, $20. SWP Paint Standardization Reference Manual for Authorized Bottlers of Coca-Cola. Manual has 17 pages and discusses the correct paint colors, as well as silkscreening colors for their automotive and signs, $50. Bottom row: 1956 Home Decorator by Sherwin-Williams. A large 43-page manual of "how to's", as well as wonderful 1950s interior colors, $20. Evercoat Brand by The Charles William Stores, catalogue with color chips and information on all their paints, order by mail. $20.

Dutch Boy Painter Magazine, May-June 1926, $12; 1920, $12.

Dutch Boy Painter Magazine, December 1928, $12.

Various paint chip foldouts, $5 each.

Various paint chip foldouts, $5 each.

Various paint chip foldouts, $5 each.

Various paint chip foldouts, $5 each.

Various paint chip foldouts, $5 each.

Various paint chip foldouts, $5 each.
Dinah Black foldout, $15.

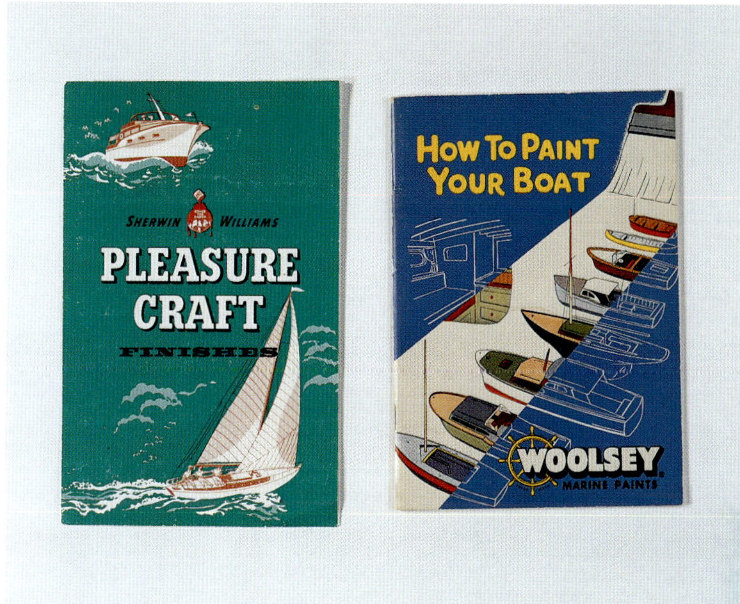

Sherwin-Williams & Woolsey booklets on painting your boat, $15 each.

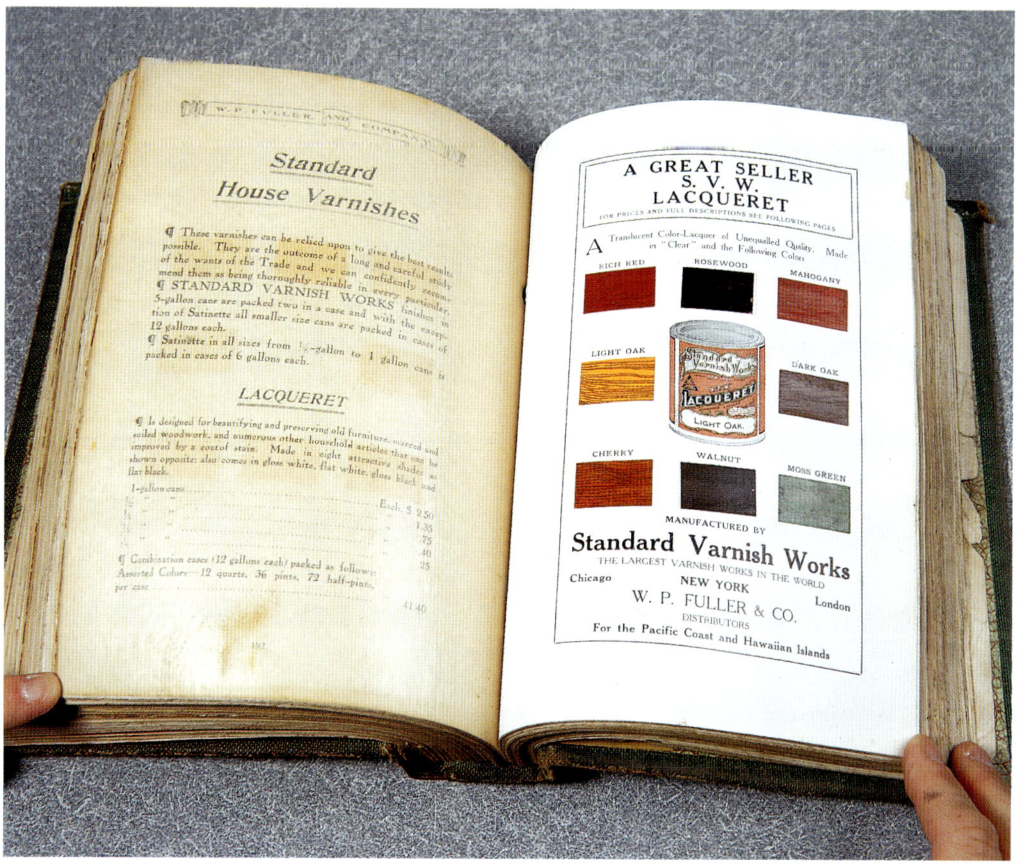

W. P. Fuller & Co. catalogue, 381 pages with pictures of all of their paint cans and color chips, $45.

Miscellanous Booklets. Includes ideas for room decorations & home designs, 1935, 1937, and 1939, $10 each.

Six different Dutch Boy blotters, $10 each.

Dutch Boy postcard, 1910, $15.

Dutch Boy blotter, $10.

Various Davis Paint Products blotters, $5 each.

Various company blotters, full color, $10 each.

Various paint company blotters, $10 each.

Sherwin-Williams Paints & Varnishes, large blotter, $15.

Various trade cards from paint companies, $15 each.

Die-cut paint trade cards, $25 each.

Fan (missing stick) picturing Miss St. Louis, Charlotte Nash, "Most Popular & Favorite Atlantic City Pageant". Back side advertises Rocklustre Varnishes and Enamels, $25.

Rev Satin Paint, fan pull, $15.

"I'se Dinah Black" fold out advertisement, "I'se de Trade Mark". Makers of Kyanize, photo shows inside and out, $50.

Photos showing before and after photos of updated storefront, to entice store owners to update their own display areas, $10 each.

Chapter Four
Small Collectibles

Giveaways & Novelties

Dutch Boy, figural match holder with original cardboard box, 6.5" tall, MIB, $450.

Boydell Bros., match holder with striker, partial 1908 calendar. Note advertising under calendar. 5" x 8", NM, $450.

Stag Prepared Paint, match holder with striker, 5" tall, exc., $125.

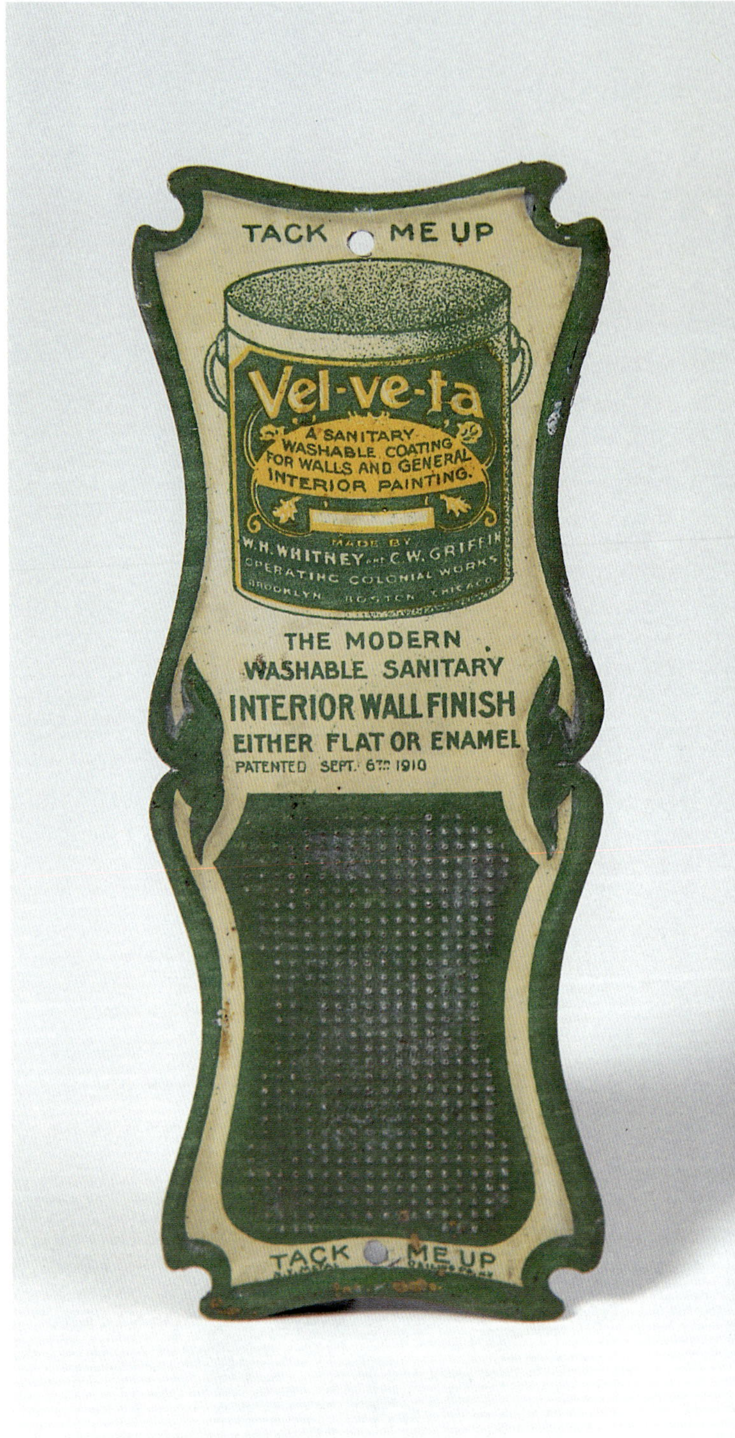

Vel-ve-ta match striker, patent dated Sept. 6, 1910, 5" tall, exc., $200.

The Billings-Chapin Paints, match holder with striker, 3.38" x 5", exc., $350.

Heath & Milligan Paints, "Sunshine Finishes".
Tip tray, 4.375" diameter, NM, $575.

Stag Semi-Paste Paint, "One Gallon Makes Two". Tip tray, 4.25" diameter, NM, $625.

Standard Mixed Paints of America,"Goes Farthest, Looks Best, Wears Longest". Heath & Milligan Mfg. Co., tip tray, 4.25" diameter, exc., $400.

Shingoleen, "The Most Efficient Shingle Finish", British America Paint Co., tip tray, 4" diameter, exc., $375.

Stag Brand Paints and Stains. Hirshberg Paint Co. tip tray, 4.25" diameter, exc., $350.

Berry Brothers Varnishes. Celluloid oval pocket mirror, 1.75" x 2.75", NM, $350.

Sherwin-Williams Paints & Varnishes, Celluloid round pocket mirror, 2" diameter, exc., $125.

Berry Brothers Varnishes, "Luxeberry White Enamel". Celluloid round pocket mirror, 2" diameter, NM, $175.

National Lead Company, "Manufacturers of Pure White Lead". Celluloid round mirror, 4" diameter, NM, $250.

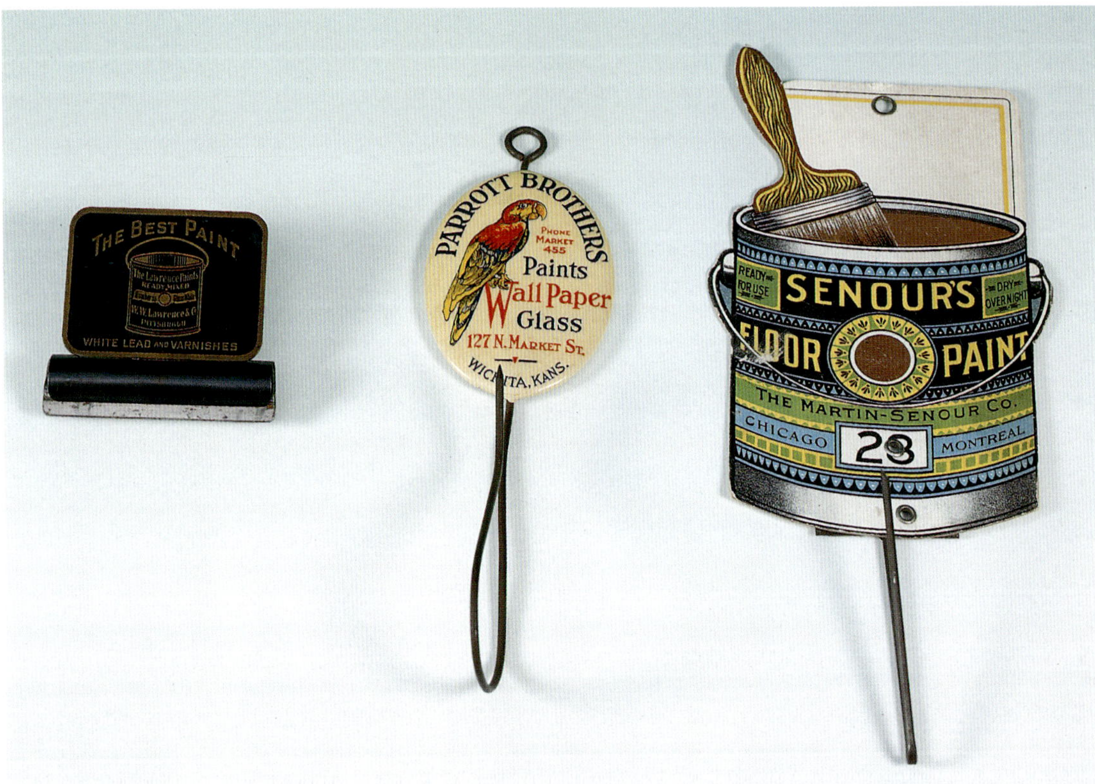

Left to right: The Best Paint, "The Lawrence Paints" bill clip, metal, 2.25" total length, exc., $45. Parrott Brothers, celluloid bill hook, 7" total length, exc., $175. Senour's Floor Paint bill hook, printed cardboard, 8.5" total length, exc., $125.

Left: Lowe Brothers Liquid-Paint, metal fob with chain, exc., $150. Right: Martin-Senour Co., "Every Drop 100% Pure". Metal fob has information about paints on back and celluloid insert, leather strap, exc., $150.

Berry Brothers Varnishes, 1903 notepad. Inside has information on their products as well as other facts such as United States population, War Revenue Tax, and Postage rates. Celluloid cover, unused, NM, $95.

Dutch Boy Heavy Duty Powdered Hand Cleanser. Avon Products, wax-coated paper container, 12-ounce size, $15.

1930 Canada Paint Company Limited. Glass paperweight with five-year calendar which rolls from inside, exc., $225.

Sargent Paint Co. Glass paperweight, exc., $95.

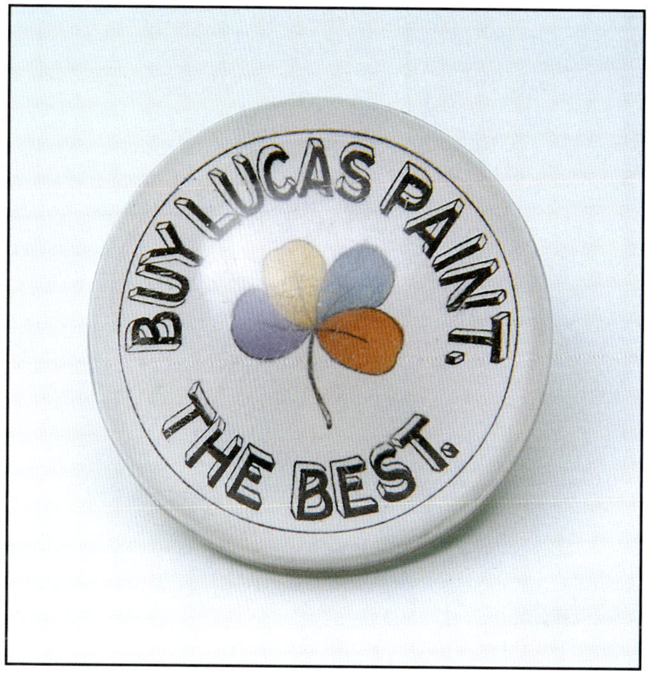

Buy Lucas Paint. Glass paperweight, NM, $85.

The Forest City Paint & Varnish Co. Glass paperweight with dice inside, exc., $175.

Edward Smith & Company Varnish-Markers, 75th Anniversary 1827-1902. Brass can paperweight, 2.5" tall, exc., $115.

Carter White Lead Co., Chicago & Omaha. Lead paperweight, 2" high, exc., $65.

National Lead Company, Perfection Anti-Friction Metal. Lead paperweight, 3.5" diameter, exc., $50.

Clockwise from left: Dutch Boy Atlantic Branch 100th Anniversary metal letter opener, 1925, 8.5" long, exc., $45. Dutch Boy black glass paperweight with pewter advertising insert, 4" diameter, NM, $95. Masury paint token, "carry me for good luck", exc., $10.

The Dutch Boy Painter. Figural metal paperweight, 4" high, NM, $125.

Left to right: Devoe & Raynolds Co. printer block, exc., $5. National Lead Company "Dutch Boy" metal letter opener, exc., $45. Sun-Proof Pittsburgh printer block, exc., $10.

The Sherwin-Williams Co. Paint and Color Makers. Metal paperweight, chameleon logo, 5.75" long, NM, $225.

Baer Brothers, "The Paint With The Two Bears, It Wears". Metal paperweight, 6" tall, exc., $175.

Left to right: John T. Lewis & Bros. Co. "Pure White Lead Old Dutch Process", celluloid pin back, 1" diameter, exc., $25. Celluloid pin back with picture of Dutch Boy, 1" diameter, exc., $15. John T. Lewis & Bros. Co., "White-Lead Linseed Oil", celluloid pin back, 1" diameter, exc., $25.

Left: Lucas Paints, celluloid pin back, 1" diameter, exc., $35. Right: Sherwin-Williams, Brighten-Up America, celluloid pin back, 1" diameter, exc., $35.

Left: Dutch Boy Quick Drying Enamel drinking glass, exc., $10. Right: Touraine Paints 50th Anniversary 1918-1968, coffee mug, NM, $20.

Eagle Pure White Lead Brush, 1924, celluloid top, mint in box, $75.

Patton's Sun Proof Paints, tin door push, 2" x 7", exc., $95.

Lincoln Paints. Pot metal tray, 3.25" long, exc., $40.

Kyanize Floor Finish. Bill hook, cardboard, 5.25" tall, exc., $100.

Save With Pittsburgh Paints—Smooth as Glass. Embossed glass bank, shaped like house, painted, exc.,$135; unpainted exc., $85.

Save With Pittsburgh Paints—Smooth as Glass. Embossed glass bank, mint, $75.

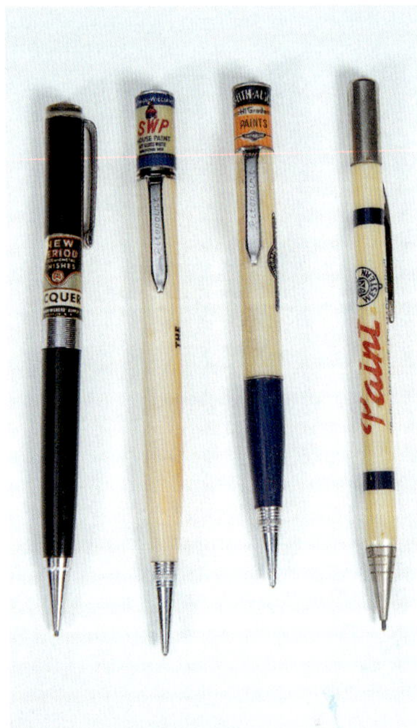

Mechanical Lead Pencils, left to right: New Period Lacquer, exc., $15. SWP House Paint, exc., $25. Smith-Alosp Paint, exc., $25. Great Western Paint, exc., $15.

Mechancial Lead Pencils. Left: Sinclair Paint, paint can top with bail handle, exc., $35. Right: Dutch Boy, paint can top, exc., $20.

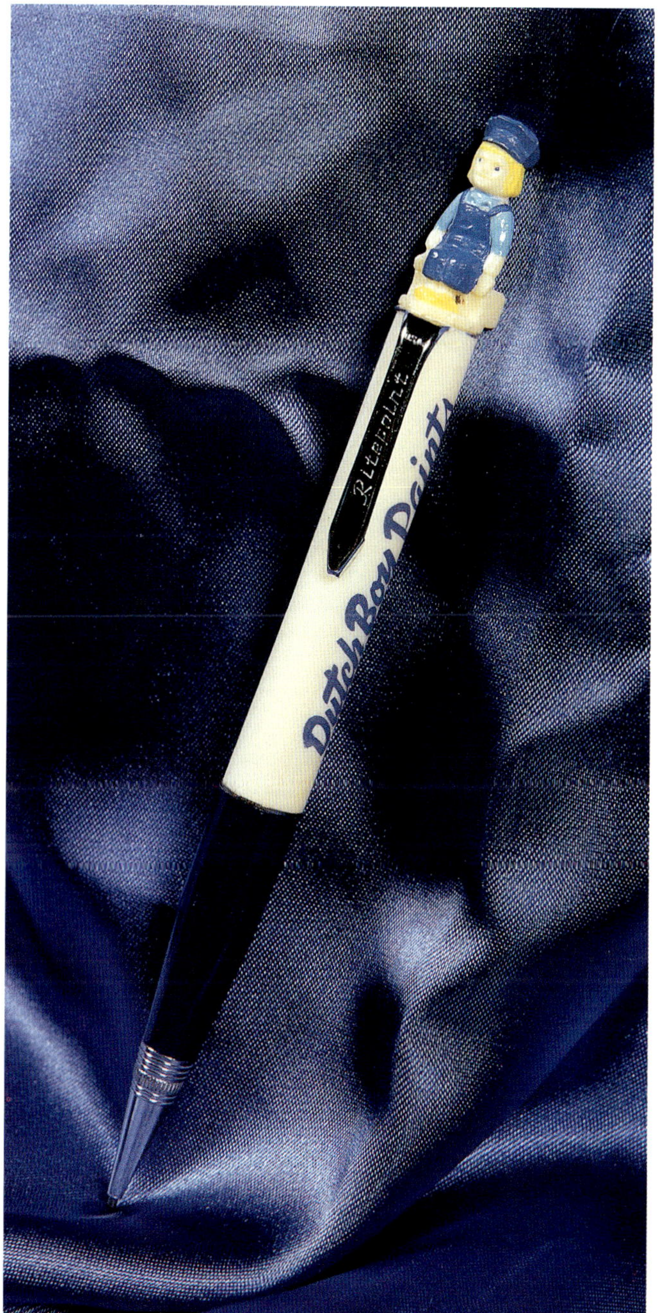

Dutch Boy Mechanical Lead Pencil. Made by Ritepoint, plastic figural Dutch Boy on end of pencil, exc., $125.

Candy Tins: Gray-Seal Paint Drops, Hard Mixed Candy. Progress Paint Mfg. Co., paper label, 1/2-pint can $20; quart size $25.

Gray-Seal Paint Golden Anniversary 1962, china ashtray, NM, $20.

National Lead Company "Dutch Boy" 1957 Safety Award, 1,000,000 Man Hours—No Lost Time. Ashtray, NM, $30.

Above: M. Buten & Son Paints and Glass, matches, exc., $25.
Below: Dentons Furniture Stores, Pittsburgh Paints, Harrisonburg, Virginia, glass ashtray, exc., $10.

Allentown Paint Products, glass ashtray, exc., $10.

Matchbooks. Left: Napko, exc, $15. Right: Merkin, with foldout 3-D display, exc., $25.

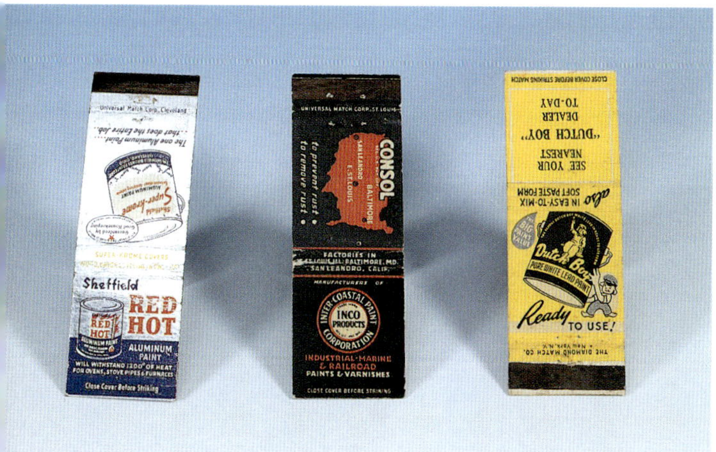

Matchbooks, left to right: Sheffield Red Hot Aluminum Paint, exc., $3. Inter-Coastal Paint Corporation, exc., $3. Dutch Boy Pure White Lead Paint, exc., $5.

Matchbooks, left to right: Dutch Boy Color Gallery, exc., $5. Dutch Boy House Paint, exc., $3. Dutch Boy Wonsover, exc., $3. Dutch Boy Nalplex, exc., $3.

Fifteen miscellaneous match pads, $3-5 each.

D & B High Grade Paint. Match container with original matches and striker on bottom, NM, $30.

Left: Du Pont Pratt & Lambert, Merritt's Paint Store, "Wind Master" lighter in box, exc., $75. Right: Dean and Barry Paint, Dundee Lighter, exc., $75.

Lighters, left to right: Tulsa Paint, Benjamin Moore Paint, Barlow miniature, exc., $40. "A Fine Name in Paint For Over Fifty Years", Smith-Alsop, Hessta in box, MIB, $40. Stan-Gard Standard Paint, Zippo, exc., $45.

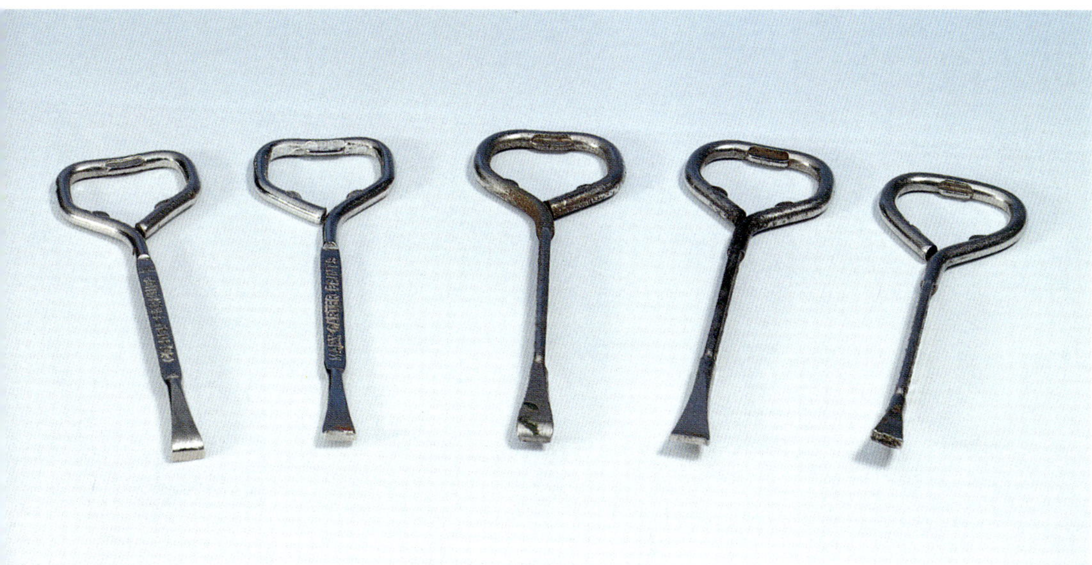

Miscellaneous paint can openers, exc., $2 each.

Top to bottom: Pittsburgh Products, Sharpening stone with box, 9" long, MIB, $10. Lucas Tinted Gloss Paint, wooden ruler, exc., $2. C.M. Athey Paint Co., large paint paddle, 13", exc., $2. Morwear Paints, paper scraper, 10", exc., $15. Canby C. Mammele, Inc., paint paddle, 9", exc., $3.

Left to right: Benjamin Moore, sewing kit, exc., $25. Benjamin Moore, key tag, exc., $15. Sherwin-Williams, tape measure (mini tape), "Barlow" (manufacturer), exc., $35. Davis Paints, celluloid key chain, 1.75" long, exc., $25.

Left: Cook's Paint & Varnish, two decks of playing cards in original box, "Congress" (manufacturer), MIB, $25. Right: Gambles Home Guard, sewing needles, 6", mint, $25.

Felton Sibley House Paint. Blank key with key ring, MIB, $20.

Hempel Marine Paint key ring, chain, and fob, MIB, $20

Chi-Namel, ladies' stick pin, copper color, exc., $35.

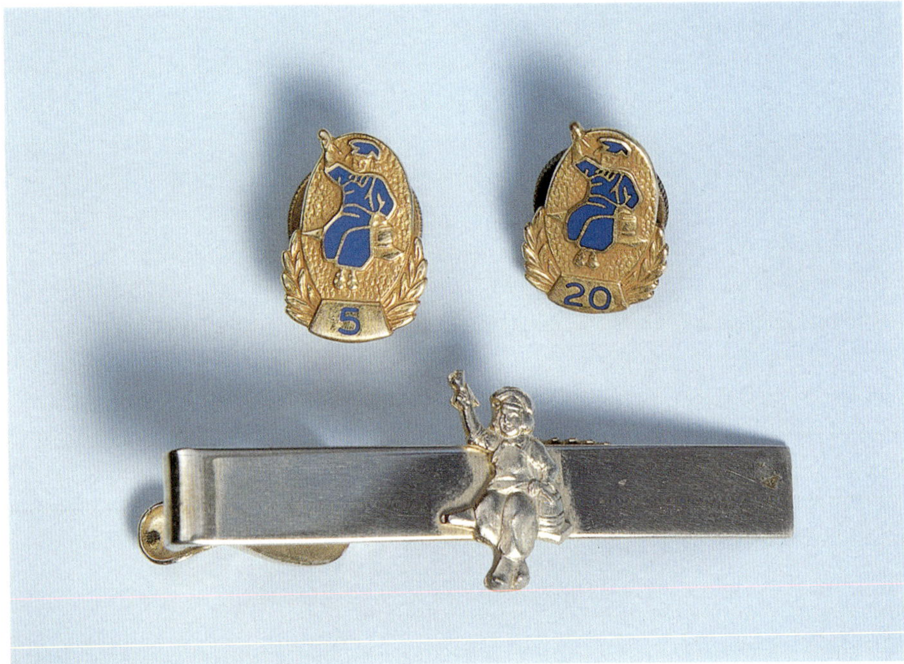

Above: Dutch Boy, 5-year service pin, exc., $30. 20-year service pin, exc., $40. Below: Tie bar, exc., $15.

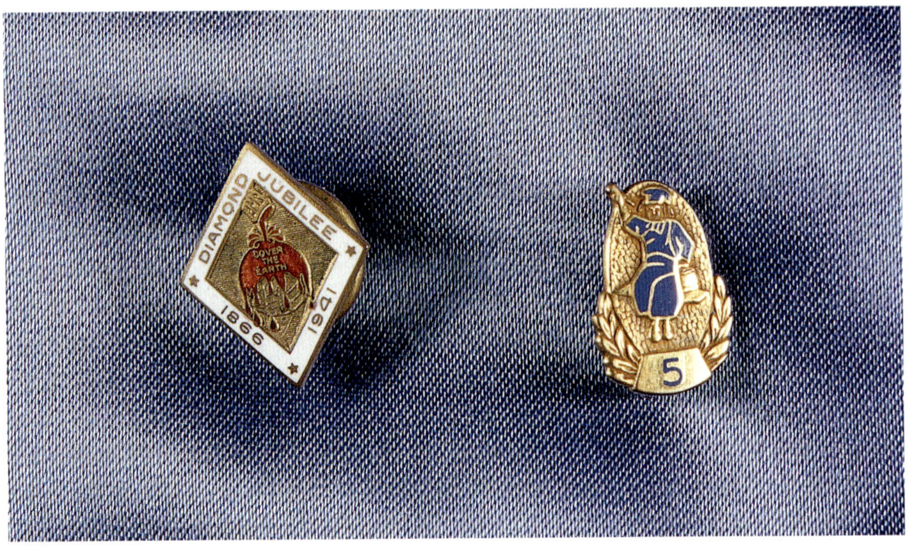

Left: Sherwin-Williams Diamond Jubilee, 1866 to 1941, exc., $25.
Right: Dutch Boy service pin, exc., $30.

Dutch Boy token, $5.

Left: Patton's Sun-Proof Liquid Paints. Patton Paint Co., printed litho label, removable top, wire bail handle, 1 1/4" high, $75. Right: Kuhn's Prepared Paint. Kuhn Paint & Varnish Works, printed litho label, sealed container, wire bail handle, 2" high, $50.

Banks

Left: Lucas, A Superior Paint For Every Purpose; tin litho, $15. Center: Lasting Paints For Every Purpose; tin litho, $25. Right: Save Everyday At Standard Brands Paint & Home Decorating Centers; $25.

Left to right: Lowe Brothers High Standard House Paint; tin litho, $20. Mr. Brush and Red Devil; paper label, $20. Mary Carter Paints, America's Greatest Values; tin litho, $15. The Country Gentleman Paints; tin litho, $20.

Left: Martin-Senour Paints, Varnishes, Enamels; tin litho, $75. Right: The Eagle-Picher Lead Company; tin litho, $75.

Left to right: Save With Cilux Enamel; tin litho, $45. Athey's Marine Finish; paper label, $25. Master-Mixed Flat Wall Finish; tin litho, $20.

Left: Patton's Sun-Proof Liquid Paints; handle missing, $85. Right: Pittsburgh Paint Products, Paint-Enamel For Every Purpose; paper label, $125.

Left: Sapolin Savings Bank; paper label, $75. Right: Monarch Paint, tin litho, $95.

Left: Black Diamond Paint & Varnish Works; barrel-shaped bank with paper label, $95. Right: Express and Delivery Wagon Colors, paper label, $20.

Left: Kuhn's Climatized Paints, litho tin, $95. Right: Varcraft Paint Products, paper label, $35.

A.P.C. American Flat Enamel Paints; 6.5" high, different colors shown, $25. Cronan "Bank on Du Pont"; 6.5" high, $25.

Left to right: De-Vo-Ko; 3.5" tall, $25. Diamond Vogel; 3.5" tall with box, $50. Dutch Boy Architectural Finishes; 3.5" tall with box, $50. Dutch Boy Dirt Fighter; 3.5" tall, $25.

Left: British Paints, 4 Seasons; 3.5" tall, $35. Right: Pro's Choice, Pro Kote; 4" tall, $25.

Left: Jones-Blair House Paint; 3.5" tall, $25. Gilman Gilplex Flat Wall; 3.5" tall, $35. Cook Wall & Trim Paint; 3.5" tall, $35.

Dutch Boy. Left: Paint book, 1929, $25. Right: "Disneyland" coloring book, 1957, $15.

Mr. Peanut watercolor set, 9.5", $95.

Devoe, tin litho watercolor box with watercolors, $45.

The Martin-Senour Co., Pioneers of Pure Paint; top, $85.

Dutch Boy Painter, Pure White Lead; board game piece, $10.

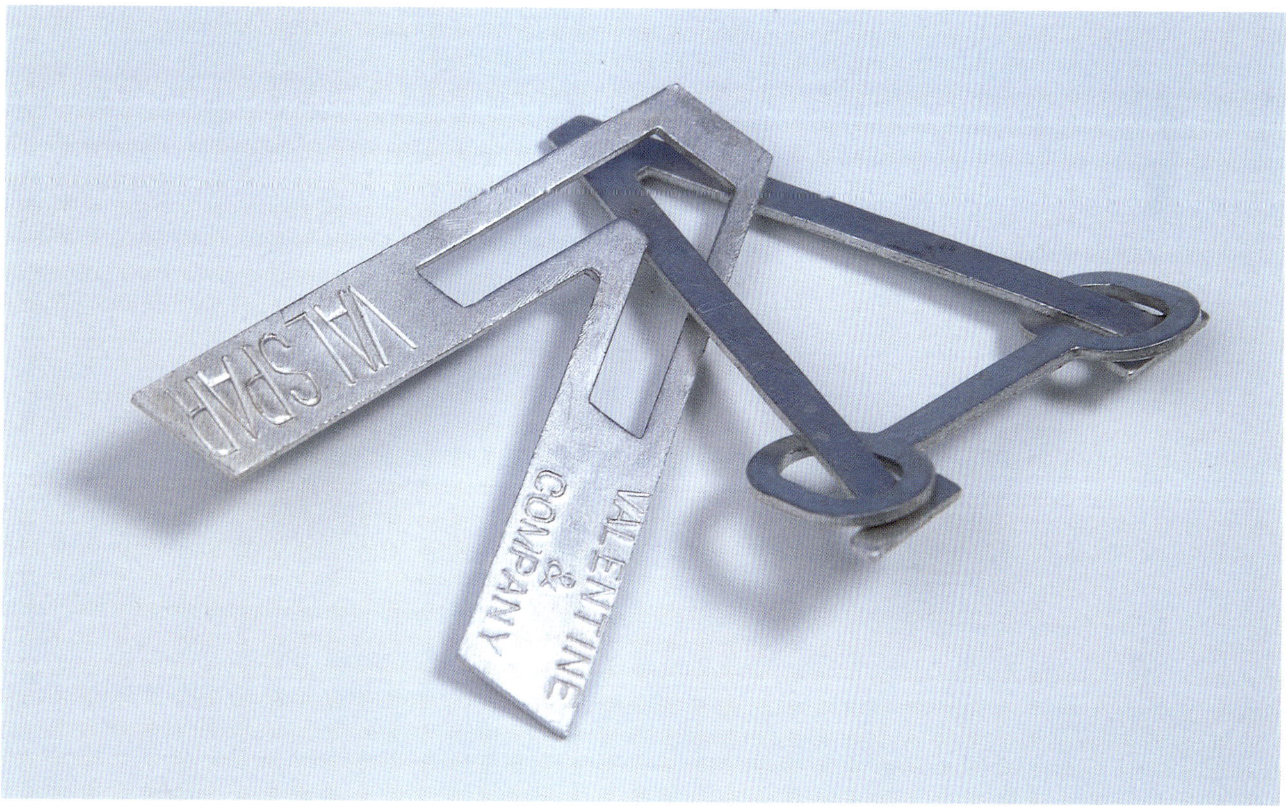

Valentine & Company, Valspar puzzle, $15.

Dutch Boy; hand puppet with original bag, $35.

Dutch Boy; large cloth doll approx. 36" tall with hard plastic hands and Dutch shoes, mask-type face with yarn hair, $175.

Chief Paint, paper headdress giveaway for children, $10.

Benjamin Moore & Co. Varnish Makers. Child's wooden wagon, 32" x 19.75", $975.

Berry Brothers Varnishes. Child's wooden wagon, 28.5" x 19.5", $900.

Sherwin-Williams Paint, wooden puzzle with paper litho. Reverse side has a United States puzzle. Complete with storage box, $275.

Dutch Boy Paints; tin litho tractor and trailer, 12.5" long, 1960s, $350.

Dutch Boy, Rollin' Across America. Nylint GMC, NRFB, $125.

Ideal Painting Decorating. Doors, ladders & paints are missing. 1950s, 11.5" long, $25 as is condition, $175 complete.

Diamond Vogel Paints, Ertl, 10.5" long, $65.

Baltimore Paint & Chemical Corporation, Winross, 9.5" long, 1979, $45.

Sherwin Williams, American Highway Legends; 11" including box, 1967, $75.

Berger Paints, Matchbox, $25.

Robin Paint & Poster Truck, Welso Toys, No. 708. Made in Great Britain, 4" x 6" long, ladders missing, $150.

Patton's Sun-Proof Paints. Child's umbrella, 21" diameter when open, exc., $395.

Chapter Five

Paint-Related Items

Left: Valentine, $10. Right: Die Cut Valentine, $20.

Whiting-Adams Brushes. Celluloid pocket mirror, 2.25" diameter, exc., $250.

Brushes by Baker. Tin display rack shaped like house, NM, $250.

Betts' Sanitary Paint Cleaner, 5-pound can., exc., $25.

Occupational shaving mugs, $350 each.

Bill Distributor and Sign Painter pin. Dated May 1920, $25.

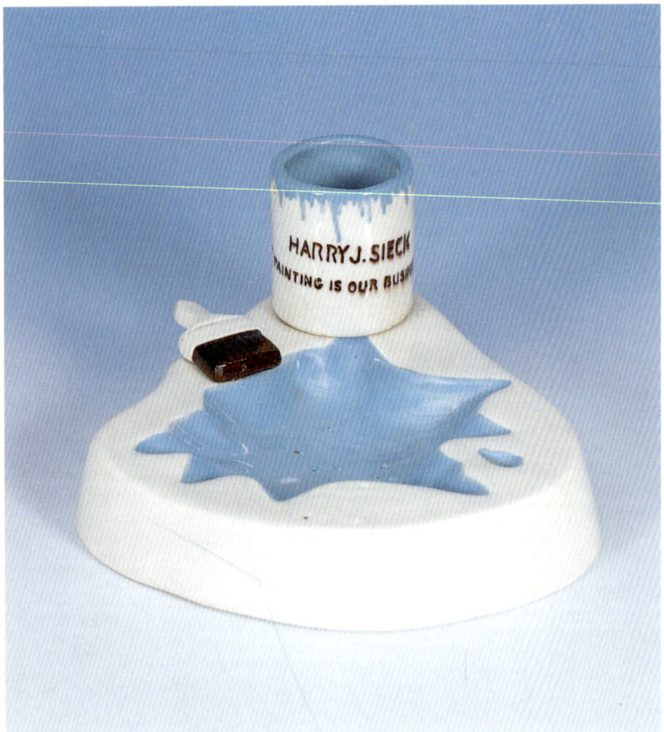

Harry J. Sieck, "Painting is our Business". Ceramic ashtray, $75.

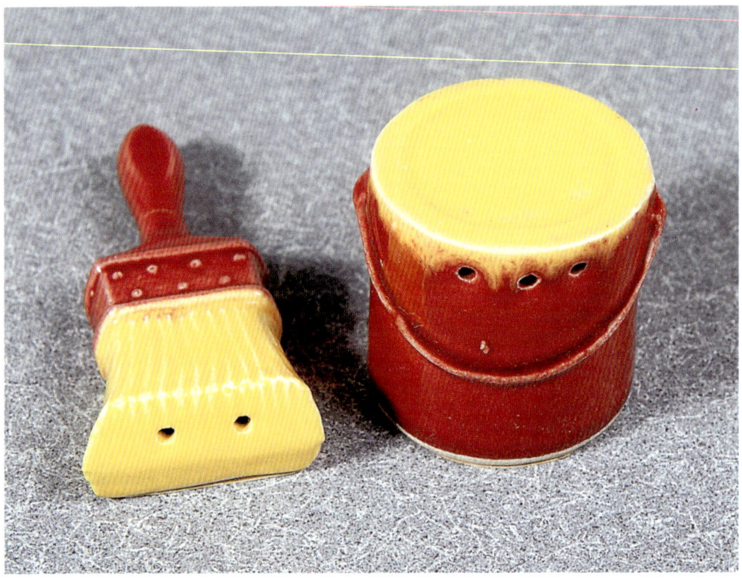

Figural salt and pepper shakers, $15.

Bibliography

Silverman, Steve. *Useless Information,* http//www.home.nycap.rr.com/useless/paint/paint.html, 1999.

National Paint & Coatings Association. *History of Paints and Coatings,* http://www.paint.org/ind_info/history.htm, 1999.